DEADLY GREED

by

Clark Cox

The McEachern Murders
in Hamlet, North Carolina

Published in the United States by:
High Country Publishers, Ltd.
197 New Market Center #135
Boone, NC 28607
(828) 964-0590
Fax: (828) 262-1973
www.highcountrypublishers.com

Library of Congress Cataloging-in-Publication Data

Cox, Clark, 1943-
 Deadly greed : the McEachern murders in Hamlet, North Carolina /
by Clark Cox.
      p. cm.
Includes bibliographical references and index.
  ISBN 1-932158-49-9 (pbk. : alk. paper)
  1. McEachern, Maceo Raines, 1946-1991. 2. McEachern, Vela,
1907-1991.
  3. Caldwell, Joey Dean, 1956-1993. 4. Murder—North Carolina—
Hamlet.
  5. Murder—Investigation—North Carolina—Hamlet. I. Title.
  HV6534.H16C69 2003
  364.15'23'0975634—dc21

2003008333

I dedicate this book to my wife, Helen Parks Cox; my children, Candice Cox and Tom Cox; my sister, Carolyn Cox Wood; and my parents, Juanita Weiss Cox and the late Scott Joseph Cox, whose lives have been a model for me and who gave me the early inspiration for a satisfying and rewarding lifelong career as a writer.

ACKNOWLEDGMENTS

Quotations in this book are exact, and nothing is "re-created" for the sake of verisimilitude. All quotations are taken from either: my notes, recorded as the person was speaking; the nearly contemporaneous recollections of those who are quoted or those to whom the quotations were delivered; or court transcripts.

The quotations from the audiotape of the "wire" worn by Bobbie Caldwell on the day of Joey Caldwell's arrest are taken from my own understanding of the words on the tape as it was played in court during Joey Caldwell's trial, not from the SBI transcript of the tape.

Bobbie Caldwell declined to be interviewed. All quotations from her are taken from the transcript of her court testimony, or from words attested to by those to whom she spoke.

In two instances, I changed names that were obviously incorrect in the court transcript. SBI Special Agent Janie Swain is referred to in the transcript as "Agent Wayne," and the Casual Lassie store where Bobbie Caldwell bought cosmetics on the night of the murders is called "Casual Massey" in the transcript.

All quotations attributed to Joey Caldwell are taken from court transcripts or the accounts of those to whom he spoke. Where I attribute an action or a state of mind to Caldwell when he was alone or in the presence of the McEacherns, I base my interpretations on Bobbie Caldwell's court testimony and/or her statements to investigators. Bobbie was Joey's sole confidante for the last five years of his life; they spent most of their time together — and even when they were apart, apparently he told her everything he was thinking and everything that he did. The sole exception, perhaps, was the plan that many lawmen believe he was considering in the weeks before his arrest: to murder Bobbie for her life insurance.

Clyde Sullivan, in the years between the murders and his suicide, declined to be interviewed — even, in the two years prior to Joey Caldwell's arrest, in the interest of clearing his own name. I have always wondered why he chose to remain silent, since, apart from Joey and Bobbie Caldwell, he was in the best position — as the only other suspect — to know that Joey Caldwell had killed the McEacherns.

Three who were interviewed for the book —Naomi Daggs, Terry Moore, and Glenn Sumpter — gave many hours to telling their stories, confirming facts, and putting me in touch with others who needed to be interviewed.

Ric Buckner gave me court transcripts and his legal expertise, filling me in on the finer points of the law in the Caldwells' trials and fleshing out my knowledge of the life insurance aspect of the murders.

Hank Drake was helpful on points of legal strategy.

Voit Gilmore helped me understand the ecology and landforms of the Sandhills.

Halbert Jackson gave me insight into race relations in Richmond County.

Wilson Moore provided insight into the day-to-day life of Richmond Countians in the 1940s.

John Hutchinson, Joe M. McLaurin, and the late J.E. and Ida Huneycutt were helpful on matters of Richmond County History. Part of Chapter II is based on material in Hutchinson's book *No Ordinary Lives: A History of Richmond County, North Carolina 1750-1900* (Virginia Beach, VA: The Donning Company, 1998).

Others who helped are named in the text.

This book represents the facts as I understand them to be, and any errors of fact or interpretation are my own.

DEADLY GREED

Last photo of Maceo McEachern, taken in April 1991.
Photo from the collection of Naomi Daggs.

I.

APRIL 6-13, 1991

1.

On the morning of Saturday, April 6, 1991 — six days before he and his 83-year-old mother were shotgunned to death in their home near Hamlet, North Carolina — Maceo McEachern paid a visit to Richmond County Sheriff R.W. Goodman.

Goodman was a legend in North Carolina politics. Sheriff for 41 years (he was to retire in 1994, after a state-record 44 years as sheriff), he was one of the last of the old-time political bosses, wielding huge influence over local voting and handing out favors to those who supported him.

He and the 44-year-old McEachern (pronounced MAY-see-oh Mc-KAY-han) had once been political allies — a necessity for McEachern, who had been the first black person elected to the Richmond County Board of Education since the Reconstruction era and, later, the first black member of the Richmond County Board of Commissioners since Reconstruction. McEachern could count on most of the black vote in the county, but that amounted to only about 18 percent of registered voters; he could not have won election without the support of the big bloc of white Democratic votes that Goodman controlled in the overwhelmingly Democratic county of Richmond.

But McEachern angered the sheriff with his votes on a couple of key issues, and he had been defeated for re-election to the Board of Commissioners in 1982 — a defeat, he believed, that was largely the sheriff's doing. He retired from elective politics after that election, but he was proud of what he had accomplished in office and proud that he had paved the way for a number of black Richmond County officeholders in the years since 1982.

McEachern had no desire to run for office again: He could no longer spare the time away from his business obligations. He and his mother, Vela McEachern, owned and operated funeral homes in both Hamlet and Rockingham, and Maceo was chief mortician for the McEachern Funeral Homes. He also had a number of other business interests, including horses and, at one time, an Amway dealership.

Goodman had supported a number of other black candidates for office, and he and Maceo remained friendly, a relationship born out of grudging mutual admiration and respect.

Goodman left the day-to-day operations of his department to Dale Furr, the chief deputy who doubled as Goodman's chauffeur, driving the sheriff's gold-colored Lincoln Continental to lunch at Wendy's or the Holiday Restaurant, to funerals, and to meetings of the boards of various businesses and public institutions. The sheriff rarely made an appearance in the Sheriff's Department, but Furr reported to him several times a day and Goodman was certain to show up at the scenes of high-profile crimes and arrests — and, through his network of political cronies and informants, he seemed to know everything that was going on in Richmond County.

He often held unofficial court on a sofa near the front window of his R.W. Goodman Company department store in downtown Rockingham, five miles from Hamlet. The window afforded a view of the front steps of the county courthouse directly across Franklin Street. If someone with whom Goodman wanted to talk passed by on the sidewalk, Goodman might send a store clerk racing out the door to intercept the pedestrian. But that was rarely necessary. Usually, people came to see R.W. Goodman without being beckoned.

Some came to ask for a job: Goodman also owned another store, Privette Furniture Company in Rockingham, and a textile plant situated north of town, and his political henchmen throughout the county owned a variety of businesses. Some petitioners merely wanted credit for a purchase of furniture or an appliance in his store: Goodman had built much of his political base by extending credit on easy terms to laborers in poverty-stricken Richmond County, and frequently he would overlook missed payments in return for votes. Others came to ask him to intercede with a judge on behalf of a son or daughter in trouble, or to court his favor in a political race.

Goodman always assured his petitioners that he would help, although it was a matter for debate whether he actually took the trouble to do so in many instances — or whether, in situations such as interceding with a judge, he really had the clout to accomplish anything. But it was said that, sooner or later, if you lived in Richmond County and wanted something badly enough, you would have to "sit in the window" and ask Goodman for it.

On this Saturday, Maceo sought only information from Goodman.

"I've got to testify against Clyde Sullivan soon in a court case," he told Goodman, "and I've heard he's made some threats against me. Is Clyde Sullivan a dangerous man?"

Goodman had known Clyde Sullivan, 62, for a good many years. You could hardly have been involved in politics in the North Carolina Sandhills without knowing him. Sullivan was owner of Sullivan Wholesalers, a beer and wine distributorship in neighboring Moore County, and he had been a heavy contributor to both Democratic and Republican Party causes, as well as to numerous charitable organizations.

Lately, Sullivan and his wife Barbara had become more closely linked to the Republicans. Barbara Sullivan had been a major contributor to then-Governor Jim Martin's re-election campaign in 1988. And Marilyn Quayle, wife of then-Vice President Dan Quayle, had paid a visit to Moore County in February 1991 on behalf of a Republican congressional candidate and had spent the night in the Sullivans' picturesque home on their Six Pillars Horse Farm near the resort town of Southern Pines.

Sullivan had grown up in modest circumstances, a minister's son in Wilson County, in impoverished eastern North Carolina. He attended Atlantic Christian (now Barton) College in Wilson and served with the 82nd Airborne Division at Fort Bragg, North Carolina, from 1951 to 1954, mustering out as a first lieutenant. In 1955 he married Barbara Mumaw, daughter of Lloyd Mumaw of Charlotte, a founder of Florida Steel Corporation. Fueled in part by his wife's money, Sullivan became a major beer and wine wholesaler in Fayetteville, North Carolina, near Fort Bragg, and in Moore County — which, as home of the golfing meccas Pinehurst and Southern Pines, was much more prosperous than Richmond County, its neighbor to the southwest.

"In many ways, Clyde Sullivan was a great man," said a Southern Pines acquaintance, Don McCluskey, shortly after Sullivan's death in 1996. "No one will ever know how many people he helped, how many good organizations he supported with his money."

But Sullivan, a cocky, bantam-like man with a generally cheerful demeanor, was also well known for having a volatile temper, and at least once he had been charged with assault. The story went that Sullivan, angry over a man's outbidding him at an automobile auction, had struck the man with his fists, knocking out several of the man's teeth. The case was settled by an infusion of Sullivan's money before it went to court, and the assault charge was dropped.

Goodman had heard that story, and a Rockingham accountant who had worked for Ballard Distributing Company, a beer distributorship in Hamlet, had also told him that when negotiations were going on for Sullivan to buy that company, "Some rough stuff went on."

There were other stories about Sullivan's beating up beer retailers who had stopped ordering from him. The stories may have been apocryphal, but they were illustrative of Sullivan's rough temper. Goodman had heard Sullivan referred to as a "thug" by some who were familiar with his temper tantrums and his no-nonsense business dealings.

Maceo knew some unsettling things about Sullivan, too. He had accompanied Sullivan, at the time a business associate of Maceo's, on a visit to the Charlotte office of another business associate, Joey D. Caldwell of Belmont. Sullivan had arrived at Caldwell's office armed with a handgun and accompanied by two off-duty Moore County sheriff's deputies who served him as bodyguards. During the meeting, Maceo said, Sullivan told Caldwell that, if need be, Sullivan would "call in my Special Forces buddies (who could) take care of somebody, and nobody would ever find them."

Now, Maceo was scheduled to testify for Caldwell, in a civil lawsuit that Caldwell had brought against Sullivan.

But Goodman was reassuring. Sullivan may have assaulted some people in the past, but Maceo was talking about a death threat, and Goodman did not believe that a prominent businessman like Sullivan would kill anyone. "Sullivan may talk tough, but I don't think he's the sort who would do anything to hurt you," he told Maceo.

Goodman was to remember the conversation after the murders, and he brought it to the attention of the Hamlet police.

2.

The murder of Maceo McEachern almost occurred on April 10.

Most people who knew him thought that Maceo, who had never married, still lived with his mother in her spacious brick, ranch-style home in the development known as "McEachern Forest" on the southern edge of Hamlet.

But the truth was, Maceo hardly ever spent a night there. He had an apartment in the McEachern Funeral Home in Rockingham. On Wednesday, April 10, he went to bed in his funeral-home apartment.

If he had gone to his mother's home, he would have died that night. The murderer, after waiting past midnight for him to show up at Vela McEachern's home, had given up and left.

3.

On the night of April 11, Maceo visited his longtime girlfriend Naomi Daggs, a teacher of English literature and composition at Richmond Community College in Hamlet.

They watched a telecast of the 1990 movie "Ghost," about a murdered man whose spirit protects his widow from the murderers.

"What do you think happens when people die?" Naomi asked him. "Is there an afterlife?"

"No," Maceo said. "I think people just die."

Vela McEachern
Photo from the collection of Naomi Daggs.

4.

On Friday, April 12, 1991, the morning of the day she and her son were killed, Vela McEachern had a brief conversation with a young employee, Chris Cox (no relation to the author), at the McEachern Funeral Home in Hamlet.

"I couldn't get my car out of my driveway yesterday morning," she complained, "because somebody had put this big old cinder block in the middle of the driveway. I didn't have room to drive around it. I had to get out and move it."

Cox thought the incident was odd, but he didn't give it much thought until police officers talked to him the next morning.

5.

April 12, like most days in early spring in Richmond County, dawned warm, and the sun burned away the early-morning dew before many residents of the county ventured from their homes. The day continued warm until midafternoon, when a cold front began moving through. By early evening the air had grown chilly, and most Richmond Countians who went outdoors wore sweaters or light jackets. It was not a good evening for front-porch sitting, yard work, or outdoor recreation.

Still, a number of people in the McEachern Forest neighborhood, as well as several passing motorists on nearby Highway 38, saw a man standing near the McEachern driveway at 103 Willow Lane late in the afternoon and early in the evening of April 12. One of the motorists, coincidentally, had come to Hamlet from Maryland that day to attend the funeral of the woman whose body Maceo was now preparing for burial.

Residents of the neighborhood saw the man standing there as they drove home from work, because Vela McEachern's house was the nearest in the development to the highway, so that others who lived there had to drive past it to get home. At least one McEachern Forest resident passed by on foot and got a close-up look. The man was dressed oddly, and that called attention to him quite apart from the curiosity of seeing a white man standing around in McEachern Forest. He wore a hunter's camouflage outfit, a camouflage hat with a floppy brim that hung down over his forehead, and floppy black boots. His hair was visible below the hat in back, and some witnesses described it as "sandy" in color. Actually, it was black, with hints of gray — but it is possible that he had dyed it for the evening. He stood next to a dark green late-model car — so dark in color as to appear almost black — that most observers described as a Honda, with an Ontario, Canada, license plate. Some noticed that the brand name and emblem of the car were covered over with what appeared to be brown package sealing tape. The trunk lid of the car was raised.

About 6:30 p.m., the man entered Vela McEachern's house. Accounts of how he gained entry differ. A confidante of the man said that he had taken a long box from the trunk of his car, knocked on the door, and gained entry by telling Vela — who was acquainted with him — that the box contained samples of a product that he hoped Maceo would agree to distribute to retailers for him. Inside the house, later that night, police found the hat and fur coat that Vela had been wearing that day laid out neatly on the bed in her bedroom — an indication that the man had used force against her only after gaining entry.

But police also found Vela's mail lying on the trunk of her white Lincoln automobile in the carport — which could have meant that the intruder had surprised her after she drove up and forced her into the house. In any case, neither the murderer nor his confidante was known for veracity, and one or both might not have told the complete truth about what happened that night.

If Vela had been home when the man arrived, why did he stand by the driveway for over an hour before going to the door, allowing numerous people to observe him?

It is more likely that he was waiting for Vela to come home.

The box contained a handgun and a double-barreled shotgun.

6.

Naomi Daggs left her job at Richmond Community College shortly before 4 p.m. and drove to Rockingham, where she worked out regularly at Slender World, a women's exercise gym. Naomi, a light-skinned black woman of 49, had been waging war against a weight problem for years, and the Slender World workouts were one battle in the war.

After she left Slender World about 5 o'clock, she drove to the McEachern Funeral Home in Rockingham to visit Maceo. The night before, he had said that he would have a body to prepare for burial the next evening, and that afterward he would

Naomi Daggs, 2000
Photo from the collection of Naomi Daggs

meet her at her home for a late dinner. She wanted to ask him what he wanted for dinner.

His answer was no surprise: He wanted pork chops, his favorite food, and he gave her money to buy the chops.

Then, unexpectedly, he picked a quarrel with her.

"It was one of those things that you can never remember clearly afterward, because it just didn't make sense," Naomi later said. "I can't remember how the quarrel started, or what it was about. I do remember that he became so angry that he banged his hand on a door frame and said, 'You've never supported me in this drink thing' — which was just silly, because I had always supported him in all his business endeavors."

The "drink thing" was Maceo's controlling interest in Pro-Formance — a "sports drink" formulated by Joey Caldwell of Belmont, North Carolina. Pro-Formance was basically spring water to which a variety of flavorings and performance-boosting vitamins and minerals had been added, making it similar to Gatorade and other sports drinks — but lower in sodium and, Caldwell claimed, with a better taste. When Caldwell decided to sell name, trademark and distributorship rights to his formulation, Maceo had battled Clyde Sullivan for the rights and won. Now, Caldwell was claiming that during the time when Sullivan was in charge of distributing Pro-Formance, he had refused to fill orders for the drink, drying up Caldwell's cash flow, in order to force Caldwell to cut Sullivan a better deal; and Maceo was soon to testify in Caldwell's lawsuit against Sullivan.

"Maceo had been worried for some time about the drink business," Naomi said. "I got the impression, though, that he was not as worried about testifying against Sullivan as he was about getting the money together to make the payments to Joey Caldwell for the distributorship rights."

Maceo had placed Pro-Formance in a number of area groceries and convenience stores and had scored a coup by placing it in the Post Exchange at mammoth

Fort Bragg, 50 miles away. But the deal had not yet started to show a profit for him — and with his horses and other investments, Maceo was cash-poor.

When he accused Naomi of not being supportive in "this drink thing," Naomi lost her temper. She threw the pork-chop money at him, saying, "Just keep the money!" She turned on her heel and left.

Instead of driving home, though, she decided to "drive around for a while and cool off." She drove for what she later estimated was about 20 minutes, then set out for the funeral home for another talk with Maceo.

Maceo wasn't there.

Naomi left the funeral home, drove down East Washington Street to Long Drive, and took Long Drive to Richmond Memorial Hospital, where she would turn left onto County Home Road, the street where she lived in a rented duplex. Near County Home Road, she saw Maceo's Lincoln automobile ahead of her. "He had told me that he had somewhere else he had to go before he finished dressing the body, and I thought he might be going on whatever that errand was," Naomi said, "but I hoped he was going to my home."

Maceo's car turned onto County Home Road. Naomi, fearful that he would see that her car was not at home and leave, drove faster than the speed limit on the narrow residential road, hoping to get there in time to talk with him. She found Maceo sitting in his car in her driveway, waiting for her. She parked her car beside his, got out and knelt by the driver's-side window of the Lincoln.

"Ma-Ma," Maceo said, using the pet name for her he had appropriated from her granddaughter Maleka, "I'm sorry. It's just that I've been so worried."

Naomi was crying. She pulled off her glasses to wipe the tears from them.

Maceo held out the money she had thrown at him at the funeral home. "Go ahead and take this money, and get those pork chops," he said.

He told Naomi that he had to go "somewhere else," but that he would come back to Rockingham while a hairdresser finished setting the dead woman's hair, he would dress her body, and then he'd come to Naomi's house for dinner.

"I know I'm selfish, but you know I love you," he told her.

"That has been a comfort to me, to have had that conversation," Naomi said. "It's helped me bear up even in the face of some doubtful things I found out about Maceo afterward — about his two-year affair with another woman, named Paulette, for example. Maceo loved women, but I was the constant in his life, and the last words he said to me were 'I love you.' "

When Maceo left Naomi's driveway he turned left, toward Rockingham, headed back to the funeral home.

"The azaleas were in bloom that April," Naomi recalled ten years later. "In all the years that I lived in that duplex after the murders, I dreaded spring. I'd look up on the hill and see Pat Swink's azaleas in bloom, and I'd think of the last night of Maceo's life."

7.

At the funeral home, Maceo answered the telephone. After talking on the phone for a moment, he rushed, telling co-workers, "I've got to go to Mama's. She says she's sick."

Co-workers later recalled that it was about 7 p.m. when he received the call. When Maceo hadn't returned by about 8:30 p.m., and Chris Cox's telephone calls to the McEachern home were not answered, Cox asked a co-worker, Clyde Harrington, to go and check on the McEacherns. Harrington drove to McEachern Forest, observing Maceo's and Velas white Lincolns in the driveway and in the carport respectively, but no other vehicles on the premises. He repeatedly knocked on the front door of the house, but his knocks went unanswered. As he made his way to a back door, he noticed that the curtains on a window in the McEacherns' den were drawn back. He peered through the window and saw Maceo — still wearing the blue jeans and starched white shirt, open at the neck, that he had been wearing at the funeral home — slumped over on a sofa, his left side to the window. Harrington called out to Maceo and rapped on the window, but Maceo did not move.

Harrington, an elderly man with high blood pressure and a heart condition, was shocked at what he had been able to see through the window. His heart pounded and his pulse raced. "I thought that thing (seeing Maceo slumped over, apparently in death) was going to take me away from here," he later said. He was to recover from his shock only after hospitalization.

But Harrington managed to report back to the funeral home, and Cox called police.

Vela McEachern's house in McEachern Forest where the murders occurred
Photo by Clark Cox

It was 9:18 p.m. Hamlet police dispatcher Martheia Fairley took the call and radioed for officers to go to the McEachern home.

8.

Hamlet police officer Gary McDonald was the first to respond to the call. McDonald opened the screen door to the McEacherns' screened-in back porch, walked across the porch, and found the back door to the house unlocked. He opened it and looked inside. He could see through to the den, where Maceo was visible on the sofa, a huge gunshot wound in his chest.

Police Sgt. Buddy Miller, who had arrived at the scene just after McDonald, stepped inside. "There's a female in the corner of the den. She's got a gunshot wound, too," he told McDonald.

The officers radioed for backup, fearing that the murderer was still in the house. Richmond County Sheriff's Deputy Nathan Grant, State Highway Patrol Sergeant Mike Valentine, and members of the Hamlet Rescue Squad responded to the call.

The law enforcement officers quickly determined that the McEacherns were dead. They searched the house and found no one else. They did find that a telephone wire in the kitchen of the house had been yanked out of the wall.

9.

Terry Moore is coordinator of Evening Guided Studies at Richmond Technical College, and he spends most of his days now with students, teachers and college administrators. Before his retirement in 1999, he was chief of police in Hamlet, but he rarely talks with his former cohorts.

"If I started getting together with them for lunch and bowling," he said, "the talk would soon turn to crimes, and I'd be giving them my opinions. They're better off without a civilian trying to interfere in their work, and I'm better off putting all that behind me."

Moore still has ambitions, though, of continuing his studies in criminal justice and becoming a college instructor. He still spends much of his spare time reading true-crime books and watching shows like *Investigative Reports* on television.

He is a slight man with spectacles and a bushy mustache. His build and his easygoing manner seem to fit a bookkeeper more than a police chief, but lawmen in Richmond County will tell you that he was among the best — trained at the FBI Academy in Quantico, Va., knowledgeable in all aspects of police work, with particular talents in interviewing suspects and finding evidence at a crime scene.

Police Chief Terry Moore
Photo courtesy of Hamlet Police Department

Most weeknights when he was not working, Moore could be found at Richmond Community College, taking criminal justice courses. But Friday night, for Moore, was family time. When the weather was right, he would grill steaks outdoors. He would watch television or go to a movie in Rockingham with his wife and three children, who ranged in age from six to sixteen, and later in the evening he might spend some time cataloging his mammoth collection of Civil War uniform buttons or reading a true-crime book before watching a rerun of *The Andy Griffith Show* and going to bed. Hamlet police officers had orders not to call him on a Friday night unless his presence was necessary.

On April 12, 1991, Moore had even forgone attending a special event in his community in order to be with his family. The old Hamlet Opera House, on Main Street in Hamlet, had recently been refurbished and restored to something approaching its turn-of-the-century glory, when it was the scene of stage performances and community gatherings. It was even rumored that the great operatic tenor Enrico Caruso had sung on its stage, trying out its acoustics while on a layover in Hamlet during a train trip from New York to Miami. Now the building, which had served some time as a movie theater before being closed in the mid-1970s and allowed to deteriorate, would once again be a center of community life. Moore was an amateur photographer with considerable skill — the summer before, he had put together a huge album of photos of Dustin Hoffman, Nicole Kidman, and other cast and crew members of the movie *Billy Bathgate* while it was filming in Hamlet — and he had been asked to come out this Friday night and take photos at the Springfest celebration that would open and dedicate the renovated performance hall. Most of the leading citizens of Hamlet would be there — with the conspicuous exception of Maceo McEachern, who had to work that night at the funeral home. Moore, too, had begged off.

But when he got a telephone call from Sgt. Buddy Miller, he knew he had to relinquish his family time.

"When they called and said, 'Come on out to the McEacherns' residence,' I knew it was serious," Moore said.

Miller had been reluctant to call Moore at home on a Friday night, but finally he realized that the call had to be made. Moore did not arrive at the McEachern home until shortly before 10 p.m., about forty minutes after Chris Cox's call to the police department. He found that the earlier lawmen on the scene, unfamiliar with investigative protocol, had not secured the crime scene by placing barrier tape around the house and yard and refusing to allow anyone to cross it.

Moore ordered that done now, and he called the State Bureau of Investigation, asking the agency to send its mobile crime lab to search for such trace evidence as hair, fibers, and fingerprints. He also placed a call to the Richmond County Sheriff's Department, asking that Deputy Aprille Sweatt, the department's laboratory and forensics specialist, be dispatched to the scene immediately with the department's own mobile crime lab. Finally, Moore called Doug Greene, a special agent with the SBI whose office was in Rockingham. (Following the pattern of FBI titles, all SBI agents are called "special agents.") Greene accompanied the forensic specialists when the SBI mobile lab arrived at the scene. With the Sheriff's Department mobile lab came, in addition to Sweatt, Capt. Dale Furr and Sheriff's Detectives Sam Jarrell and Harold Napier. All the top criminal investigators Richmond County had to offer were on hand, collectively representing more than a century of experience at investigating crime scenes.

Sheriff R.W. Goodman was conspicuously absent. Although he was glad enough to have his deputies dispatched to the crime scene to help out in the initial investigation, he knew that the murders, having occurred in Hamlet, were outside his department's jurisdiction.

10.

Coincidentally, many of the county's governmental and political leaders who were not at the Hamlet Opera House that night were one block up Main Street at Steeples, a former Roman Catholic church that had been converted into an upscale restaurant by Debbie Robertson, wife of the principal of Richmond Senior High School. On April 12, the restaurant had been rented for the night by a Rockingham couple who had recently been awarded custody — tantamount to adoption — of their foster daughter. The court had decided the custody suit only after a months-long battle between the foster parents and the North Carolina Department of Social Services, which wanted to return the infant to her birthmother, a 16-year-old seventh-grader with no means to care for a baby. It was the little girl's first birthday, and the parents were holding a party for all the people who had gone to bat for them in the protracted court proceeding.

Years later, the mother of the child, Helen Cox (the author's wife), would say, "Every time I see the videotape of Candice's first birthday party, I can't help but think that Maceo and his mother were being shot to death just a mile away, while we were celebrating."

Helen Cox had come to Rockingham nearly twenty years before, just out of college, and had worked briefly as society editor of the *Richmond County Daily Journal* in Rockingham. She had met Maceo at a party and, although she was white and he was black, he had taken her under his wing and introduced her to his circle of friends, both black and white. Helen considered Maceo a close friend and was devastated when, shortly after the Coxes returned home from the party, the phone rang with news of the murders.

11.

News of the murders traveled fast. Virtually everyone in Richmond County knew Maceo McEachern and his mother, and when word went out over police radio that there had been a shooting at the McEachern home, people with police scanners ran to their telephones to pass on the bad news to friends. The phone wires hummed until after midnight throughout the county, as many made re-peated calls to friends and acquaintances to ascertain just what had happened. Though they feared the worst, Richmond Countians hoped against hope to learn that the McEacherns had not been the shooting victims.

Dozens of people got into their cars and drove to McEachern Forest, to find out first-hand what had occurred.

No one called Naomi — but she sensed that something was wrong.

"Chris Cox had called me several times to ask if I had heard from Maceo," she said. "I started getting this sinking feeling, and I finally called him back to ask him if he thought I should go to Vela's house. 'Maybe you better go,' he said."

Naomi recalled that it was "at least 8 o'clock" when she set out for McEachern Forest, taking with her Carolyn Cosby, principal of West Rockingham School, who was her next-door neighbor and best friend. Actually, it must have been about 10 p.m., judging from the police chronology of events — late enough to confirm Naomi's "sinking feeling" that something was terribly wrong.

"When we got there," Naomi said, "I knew something bad had happened. There were police cars all over the place, an ambulance, and people were milling about in the yard and driveway.

"Terry Moore saw me and came to the car before I could get out. 'You can't go in,' he told me. 'You don't want to go in. They've both been shot, and they're both dead.'

"We went next door to Callie Ellison's house. To tell the truth, considering what Maceo's state of mind had been for the past few days, my first thought was that it had been a murder-suicide."

12.

Police Chief Terry Moore thought so, too, at first.

Moore, who like most people in Hamlet considered Maceo a good friend, was shocked at the condition of his friend's body. He didn't notice the chest wound at first, but he could not avoid seeing the face wound. Maceo had been shot in the mouth at close range with a shotgun. "His teeth were scattered all over the room," Moore said.

Vela, wearing a blue skirt and a blouse with black, white, and yellow horizontal stripes, her body in an easy chair facing her son's body, had also been shot in the chest and again in the head. As many shooting victims will do, she had stretched out a hand in front of her in a futile attempt to deflect the first shotgun shell. It had ripped through her hand, nearly severing her thumb.

"At first, before I took it all in, I thought I was looking at a murder-suicide," Moore said. "The shot pattern of the shotgun pellets in Maceo's face was very unusual, widely scattered vertically but very narrow horizontally, as if the gun had been discharged just beneath Maceo's chin. I saw Mike Valentine (the State Highway Patrol sergeant) carrying a shotgun, and I cried out, 'Why did you do it, Maceo?'

That's when Mike told me the shotgun was his own riot gun, and the murder weapon had not been found.

" 'Are you telling me that we have no idea who did this?' I asked him. And Mike said, 'That's right.'

"That made it an unusual crime for our small town. You have 'whodunits,' and you have 'smoking guns.' Most of the murders we investigated were smoking guns. Either you literally find the murderer standing over the body with a gun or knife in his hand, or you question the most likely suspects and make an arrest within 24 hours. Usually, the murderer is either a family member or someone the victim had a quarrel with in a tavern. But if you don't solve a murder within 24 hours, a solution becomes less likely with every day that passes."

To Moore, these murders looked like the work of a professional. The murderer had shot each victim twice, to make sure they were dead, and he had picked up and taken away the spent shells. He had ripped the telephone out of the wall, to keep the person who discovered the bodies from calling police, giving him more of a head start to escape.

Moore had difficulty keeping his mind on his work. "I couldn't help thinking that I had recently visited the McEacherns and sat right where Maceo was sitting now. I flashed back to the times I had encountered Maceo recently — at a restaurant, having lunch, or talking to him in front of the post office about crime. I remembered that he had expressed himself as being pretty strong on punishing criminals."

Moore thought that Maceo would have been particularly eager for justice in this sort of murder case. "We — all the law officers present — were put off by the idea of killing a son in front of a mother, or a mother in front of a son," he said. "Somehow that made it a few degrees worse than murder, even."

Moore closed his mind to thoughts of Maceo, as best he could, and looked for evidence.

"A strange thing happens when you're at a murder scene," he said. "After you're there for a while, looking for trace evidence, taking pictures, talking with other officers and planning your investigation, you almost get used to dead bodies being in the room with you. Then you'll come back to reality and you'll realize what a horrible scene you're in. Those flashes of reality were particularly emotional for us at the McEacherns, because the dead bodies had been people we all knew and liked and respected."

The blood spatter patterns on the walls, floor, and furniture showed that the McEacherns had died where they sat. "The patterns," Moore said, "showed that the killer had been standing almost right over them, at close range, and fired a little bit downward. You could still smell gunpowder, all over the house."

A frying pan, broken into several pieces by the force of some impact, lay at Vela's feet. A post-mortem examination later established that Vela had suffered a blow to the head. Presumably the murderer had struck her with the frying pan hard enough to shatter it.

"I called in the State Bureau of Investigation mobile laboratory almost as soon as I arrived at the scene," Moore said. "The house was full of fingerprints, as homes naturally are — but they never found any that matched up to be worth anything as evidence. There were no usable fingerprints on the frying pan, which indicated to me that the killer had worn gloves.

"And they didn't find any footprints or anything else that might give us a clue to the murderer's identity. The yard was full of grass and didn't yield any footprints. And there just wasn't any 'transfer' evidence — hair or fibers — even though the carpet in the den was worn and somewhat dirty and the forensics people took a lot of care with it, vacuuming up everything and bagging it carefully in evidence bags.

"We found one exterior door, on the southeastern corner of the house, that looked like it had a little damage to it. But our best opinion was that the damage to the door didn't have anything to do with the murders."

It didn't surprise Moore that the investigators found no good evidence. He doubted whether the police would solve these murders within a few hours, if ever. It looked to him like a contract killing, and his fear was that by the next day the murderer would be in the Cayman Islands, relaxing on the beach and counting his payoff money.

The forensics technicians took dozens of photographs throughout the house. Moore followed them, taking backup photos with a small Instamatic camera that his department owned — "just to be sure, in case the SBI photos didn't turn out for some reason."

Moore called Richmond County Medical Examiner Wendell Wells, a physician who was also Maceo's closest friend, to render an official opinion as to the cause of the McEacherns' deaths. Shaken by the news, Wells brought his wife with him as moral support. As Wells left the house after examining the bodies and announcing his verdict of deaths by homicide, he looked to some observers as if he were on the verge of collapsing.

The crime scene was already contaminated. Neighbors and friends of the McEacherns, and some curiosity seekers, had arrived shortly after they picked up the first reports of the crime on their police scanners or gotten word by telephone. They had trod through the yard, obliterating or rendering useless any of the killer's footprints that might have been left on the lawn. Some had even entered the house, although the uniformed officers and detectives had succeeded in keeping them out of the den.

"Michael McInnis (Maceo's friend and business partner in the horse farm) was there," Moore said. "Naomi was there. Glenn Sumpter (editor of the *Richmond County Daily Journal* in Rockingham) was there. I don't know how bad news travels so fast.

" Nathan Grant and I went over to a neighbor's house to ask if he had heard the shots. He hadn't. But when he asked about Maceo and his mother and we told him they were dead — well, he just basically screamed."

13.

Moore couldn't sleep that night. Instead of going home, he drove to the police station and shut himself in his office, just thinking about the murders.

This wasn't unusual for Moore. He often locked himself in his office on quiet days and spent hours poring over investigative reports and "cold case" files from years before, searching for some trace of evidence the original investigators had missed. He had solved numerous crimes in just this way during his 20 years on the force. Once, after studying a file about a man who had died an unexpected, but seemingly natural, death of a hemorrhage in the brain, Moore had gone back to the man's neighborhood, interviewed neighbors, and learned that the man had been hit on the head in a fight several days before his death. Moore arrested the other fighter and charged him with manslaughter; the man was convicted.

On the night of April 12 and the early morning of April 13, Moore said, "I kept thinking that the killer, who had planned so carefully that he didn't leave any physical evidence, had nonetheless taken a big risk. He had stood near the McEachern house for a long time, and his camouflage outfit and the car with the Canadian plate were bound to make him noticeable. He used a shotgun, which has a loud report when fired. Only the fact that it was an unseasonably cool night, and that the neighbors were inside their houses watching television with their windows closed, kept the shots from being heard. It seemed strange to me that the killer had taken such a big risk on the 'front end' of the crime, after planning it so carefully on the other end. That didn't sound like a contract killer to me. It sounded like an amateur.

"I sensed that he was getting a little desperate at this point — so desperate, for whatever reason, that he wanted to get it over with on that night, no matter what the risk. That made me think that maybe he had tried to kill the McEacherns before.

"And that brought me back to thinking about the concrete block."

Moore finally made his way home and fell into bed. But he arose early on Saturday, April 13, and went back to the McEachern house. On the way, he detoured down Highway 38 and fished through the contents of a public trash dumpster — the nearest dumpster to the McEachern house — hoping that the killer had discarded his gun or other incriminatory evidence there. He came up empty-handed.

He had noticed the large masonry block beside the driveway the night before, while trying to persuade the crowd gathered around the McEachern house to retreat behind the barrier tape. Now, Moore took a closer look at the block.

"It looked out of place to me," he said. "Maceo was not a do-it-yourselfer, and there weren't any other concrete blocks around. And this block had mud on it — red clay mud. There's no red clay in the Sandhills. That block had to have been brought there from somewhere else.

"I went to the station and told (Assistant Chief, later Chief) Robert Bristow to go get the block, bring it down to the station and lock it in the evidence vault."

Later, when he learned what Vela had told Chris Cox about the block, Moore theorized that the murderer had placed it in the driveway on the evening of April 11 — hoping that, when Maceo came home, he would have to get out of his car to move the block and the murderer could ambush him.

The theory proved to be correct, except that the block had actually been placed there on April 10. If Maceo had come to his mother's house on the evening of April 10, he would have died then — but Vela, most likely, would have lived. The murderer would have made his escape before she could get a look at him and become a witness who had to be eliminated.

That block proved to be one of the most important pieces of evidence in the case.

14.

The SBI had been on the job most of the night, and they had found a few clues, although it was too early to know how important the clues might be. They had found some plastic wadding and a few shreds of paper wrapping from the shotgun shells. These items, it turned out, proved that the shells that had killed the McEacherns were of a type that had not been manufactured for many years.

It was likely that, if the murderer had purchased the shells recently, he could have purchased them from only a limited number of stores — stores that still had the outdated ammunition in stock. This information might later help to establish where the shells had been purchased, and by whom.

Investigators had found a wallet on Maceo's body containing what Moore called "a large amount of money." Its presence ruled out robbery as a motive for the killings.

It wasn't long before the investigators started to look at Maceo's Pro-Formance drink distributorship as a possible motive.

15.

Year in and year out, Richmond County averaged about one homicide a month. In a county of roughly 45,000 people, that worked out to a murder rate more than twice that of the nation as a whole in 1991, and greater even than most major metropolitan areas.

But almost all of Richmond County's murders fell into four broad categories: murders of wives by husbands or husbands by wives, murders growing out of fights at "beer joints" or nightclubs, murders committed in the commission of (or to cover up) other crimes such as robbery, and murders related in some way to criminal conspiracies, most often drug trafficking. Most sober, honest citizens of the county, devoted to their families, could not imagine being either the perpetrators or the victims of those sorts of murders.

The murders of the McEacherns, however, were of a different kind. News of the killings sent a shock wave throughout Richmond County. Vela McEachern was one of the county's leading businesswomen, and her son was a political and business leader in his own right, in addition to being one of the most popular individuals in the county.

Two respected citizens had been murdered "execution-style" in their own home, evidently by a professional hit man, with no obvious motive — and the murderer had gotten away.

The murders had an immediate effect on behavior and attitudes throughout the county and beyond. All over Richmond County by the night of April 13, 1991, the doors of some houses were being locked at night for the first time, and people were watching their backs. No one could know who might be the next victim.

II.

RACE AND VIOLENCE

1.

Richmond County, North Carolina, may fairly be said to lie in the Deep South. The 35th parallel of north latitude, which forms the northern state lines of Georgia, Alabama, and Mississippi, divides Richmond County in two, passing a few miles north of the two largest towns, Rockingham (population about 10,000) and Hamlet (population about 5,000). The climate is warm, almost tropical during the hottest summers, and winter snows are infrequent, shallow, and of short duration.

The first Europeans — Spanish explorers — passed through the area that is now Richmond County in the 1500s, but they didn't linger and didn't return; the only sign of their passing was a badly rusted, hand-worked tempered iron rapier that two fishermen discovered near the Pee Dee River in the 1970s. The first permanent European settlers didn't arrive in the area until the 1730s, and they were English and Scottish. Native Americans had lived there for 10,000 years or more, but the few Indian inhabitants who remained in the early part of the eighteenth century wisely took the path of least resistance and moved out as the white man began to move in.

Millions of years ago, the ocean reached into and beyond the area, to the mountainous foothills of the Appalachian range. When it receded, it left behind a sandbank, over eighty inches deep, running from present-day Richmond county in south central North Carolina to Aiken and Barnwell counties along the Savannah River, in the southernmost reaches of South Carolina. Over eons, winds and erosion formed hillocks of the sand, some more than a hundred feet in depth, giving the area its characteristic appearance and its twentieth-century name: the Sandhills. The sandy soil defined the character of farming and industry in Richmond County's early history, and the plantations and cotton mills, in turn, set the tone for race relations well into the twentieth century.

2.

The first European settlers found that the sandy soil could support a wide variety of crops, particularly along the bottomlands of the rushing Pee Dee and its tributaries, where it was mixed with river loam. Shortly before the American Revolution, a planter recently arrived from England by way of Jamaica, Henry William Harrington, began experimenting on a large scale with crops of indigo and cotton. He discovered that the land and the climate were ideally suited to growing cotton — both in the Sandhills and in the northern sections of the county, where the sand gave way to the red clay of the low Uwharrie Mountains and the lower North Carolina Piedmont.

Harrington became North Carolina's highest-ranking general of militia during the war, and when Richmond County was founded in 1779, he was its first representative to the North Carolina General Assembly and was named to a three-man commission to found a county seat. The three decided to place the seat of local government on a hilltop — a huge granite outcropping covered with sandy soil, near the confluence of Hitchcock Creek and Falling Creek, the Pee Dee's two largest tributaries in the area. They laid out the first streets and building lots and named the town "Rockingham," after Charles Watson-Wentworth, Marquess of Rockingham, who had been sympathetic to the colonists' cause in the years leading up to the Revolution.

The county's early economy depended almost entirely on cotton: Some of the South's earliest cotton mills were built there, beginning in 1837 when a group of local investors ordered yarn-spinning equipment from Fall River, Massachusetts, and started up the Richmond Manufacturing Company on Falling Creek in Rockingham. Generative power for the "Richmond Mill" and the mills that followed it came from water wheels in Hitchcock Creek, Falling Creek, and two impoundments upstream on Hitchcock Creek, Roberdel Lake and Ledbetter Lake. The cotton farmers found local markets for their crops, no longer having to brave the rutted wagon roads to the port in Wilmington, North Carolina, or the treacherous boat journey down the Pee Dee to Georgetown, South Carolina. Soon, in Rockingham, the road leading to Fayetteville (and called Fayetteville Road to the present day) was lined with large, luxurious plantation homes.

3.

The cotton economy depended on slavery. In 1860, the year before the Civil War broke out, Richmond County had a population of almost 11,000, fully half of whom were slaves.

The life of a slave was harsh at best. In the 1930s, former Richmond County slave Louisa Adams told a federal Works Progress Administration interviewer (who transcribed her recollections in vernacular dialect) that, "Master worked us hard and gave us nothin'. ... Our clothes were bad, and beds were sorry. ... We got one pair o' shoes a year. When dey wored out we went barefooted. ... We lived in log houses daubed with mud. ... My brother wore his shoes out, and had none all thu winter. His feet cracked open and bled so bad you could track him by the blood."

In the cotton fields, Louisa Adams recalled, "Dey waked us time de chicken crowed, and we went to work just as soon as we could see how to make a lick wid a hoe. ... If fire wuz out or any work needed doin' around de house, we had to work on Sundays. They did not gib us Christmas or any other holidays."

Not surprisingly, some slaves rebelled. In 1831 a group of Richmond County slaves, emboldened by news of Nat Turner's Rebellion in Southampton County, Virginia, plotted a massive slave rebellion for Christmas Eve — but one of the slaves who had been asked to join the plot, ironically named Nat, turned in the others to the white authorities. Six leaders of the abortive rebellion were arrested and convicted in court, and at least one, a minister named Avery, was sentenced to death. No records survive that tell of Avery's fate, but he was probably hanged — and the other five may have followed him to the gallows. Things went even harder for the slaves after that. Another abortive slave rebellion in Richmond County in 1864, as the Civil War was winding down and it had become obvious that the South's cause was lost, resulted in the lynching of three slaves and a January 2, 1865, trial of thirteen others. Again, history does not tell us what became of the thirteen.

4.

The post-Civil War economy was largely one of textile mills and tenant farming, and the freed slaves still had to struggle to keep body and soul together: Most farmed "on shares," giving up 50 percent of their income to the white landowners, whom they also had to pay for plants, fertilizer, and equipment.

During Reconstruction, blacks held most of the public offices in Richmond County, but they kept an uneasy peace at best with the big landowners and the white textile-mill workers, many of whom fared little better than the slaves. The textile workers, well into the twentieth century, were paid largely in books of scrip that they could exchange for merchandise at the company store; the workers called them "dookie books," their vulgar estimate of the scrip's worth. The mills owned the workers' houses and charged them rent, and frequently even the workers' children were forced to labor in the mills without pay: As late as the

1940s, Rockingham folk-song writer Dorsey Dixon could write about a golf course being built adjacent to a textile mill, "So the little children could look out/ And see the grown men play."

Feelings ran high between the freed blacks and the poor whites, who felt that they were competing for the same low rungs on the ladder of the local economy.

In 1876, Rutherford B. Hayes was elected president in a hotly disputed election settled by hard bargaining in the U.S. House of Representatives. As their part of the bargain, white Southern Democrats insisted that the federal government ease Reconstruction's hold on the South. That same year, some whites from Richmond County — calling themselves "Red Shirts," because they wore red shirts like those the first Confederate Army company from the county, the Pee Dee Guards, had worn — rode on terrorist campaigns of white supremacy, discouraging blacks from voting in the South Carolina elections. The Red Shirts became inactive after the election, but many of the group's members joined the Ku Klux Klan, which sometimes held meetings on the town square in Rockingham.

The Red Shirts rode again in 1898, this time in Richmond County, and this time their shirts were emblazoned with the letters "W.S." for "white supremacy." Richmond County politics had often been violent, characterized by fistfights, riots, and even occasionally by duels, but the 1898 campaign brought the violence to a new level. Night after night, the Red Shirts, carrying guns, rode through black neighborhoods. They shot no one, but they badly beat a number of black men who dared to venture outdoors during their night rides. The Red Shirts intimidated and frightened black would-be voters, threatening horrible retribution against any who dared to vote on Election Day.

Leaders of the white supremacy movement were primarily from the southeastern section of the county, which two years later was to break off from Richmond County and form Scotland County, at least partly because of white supremacy doctrines. But a major instigator of the latest Red Shirt movement was Cameron "Cam" Morrison, former mayor of Rockingham and chairman of the county's Richmond County Democratic Party Executive Committee, who was later to move his law practice to Charlotte, adopt more moderate views on race, and become known as a "progressive" governor of the state between 1921 and 1925.

The Red Shirts' campaign of terrorism and intimidation broke the hold of the black Republicans on county government and made Richmond a solidly Democratic county — which it has remained to this day, despite the party's long since having given up the title of "the party of the white man." The last black officeholder in the county (until 1972), Justice of the Peace Harvey I. Quick, resigned the position in 1900, under intense pressure from whites.

5.

Even after the great recession of the late 1890s — the days of nickel-a-bale cotton —forced many Richmond County farmers out of the cotton-producing business (the rest were to follow by the 1950s, persuaded by the boll weevil to choose other crops), the textile mills continued to be crucial to the county's precarious economic status. But after 1897, railroads came also to play a large part in the county's fortunes.

In that year, the Seaboard Air Line Railroad (later to merge with the Atlantic Coast Line Railway to form the Seaboard Coast Line Railroad, now CSX) established its headquarters in Hamlet, a backwater town five miles from Rockingham. Rails stretched in four directions from the huge rail depot in Hamlet. Near the depot, Seaboard Air Line built maintenance shops and a roundhouse. In later years, the shops were moved several miles up Highway 177 to a giant switching yard, but the railroad remained Hamlet's chief employer.

Freight trains rumbled through Hamlet several times a day, and twice a day passenger trains rolled through — one headed north from Miami to New York, the other on its way from New York to Miami. Hamlet was a stopover on the route, and in the early part of the century almost every celebrity in the nation had eaten at one time or another in Hamlet's Terminal Café. Once, when black educator Booker T. Washington disembarked and asked to eat in the segregated café, management put up screens around the table of Washington and his party — a "separate but equal" dining area that was meant to accommodate the party under the Jim Crow laws but raised the hackles of some blacks who saw the action as condescending and discriminatory.

Hamlet became a thriving, bustling town, larger for most of the first half of the twentieth century than Rockingham, and it had plenty of work to offer laborers both black and white. There was nothing in Hamlet to compare with the antebellum plantation houses that lined Rockingham's Fayetteville Road on both sides, but Hamlet now had something that Rockingham didn't have — a large middle class. Railroad workers were skilled, unionized, and much better paid than textile workers. Their new status engendered a fierce pride in Hamlet's residents, and a spirit of competition that continues to this day, two decades since the railroad pulled out part of its shops and became less important to the town's economy.

Residents of Hamlet point with pride to the celebrities born there during the decades of railroad prosperity — including Tom Wicker, who was to become national columnist and associate editor of The New York Times; Bob Carroll, who for many years was head writer for the immensely popular "I Love Lucy" television series; Billy Harris, who played baseball briefly in the major leagues in the 1960s; and even Bill Creech, who made the "Ripley's Believe It or Not" newspaper column by hitting a home run for the Hamlet High School baseball team, though he had only one arm (he had lost the other in early childhood, when a railroad car ran over it).

There were black celebrities as well. Jazz saxophonist John Coltrane was born in Hamlet, as were major league baseball player Franklin Stubbs, who holds the Houston Astros' one-season record for home runs and played first base for the Los Angeles Dodgers when they won the World Series in 1988; Philadelphia Eagles All-NFL offensive end Mike Quick; and two other NFL players, Lewis Breeden of the Cincinnati Bengals and Perry Williams of the New York Giants, who earned Super Bowl rings.

Hamlet had three distinct black neighborhoods. One was East Hamlet, where lived laborers and a few domestic workers. One was "North Yard," between Hamlet and the rail yards, where the sturdy homes of railroad porters and stewards sat side-by-side with one-room shanties that had dirt floors and rough-hewn fireplaces for cooking and heating. In the back yards of the shanties, hand-dug wells sat in dangerous proximity to hand-dug pit privies.

On Charlotte Street, blacks lived in a row of modest homes placed back-to-back to the larger houses on Hamlet Avenue, the town's high-class white residential section. Early each morning, domestic workers from Charlotte Street would make their way to the Hamlet Avenue houses, often carrying buckets of coal to lay a fire in the fireplaces before the white families arose for the day. They worked for meager pay and "tote rights," being allowed to clean the bowls of leftovers from the white families' tables and take them home for their own families' dinners.

Many of the male residents of Charlotte Street worked for the railroad. Most were porters, "red caps" and dining attendants, while some others had higher-paying manual labor jobs in the switching yards or worked as cooks on the trains. Still others were bellmen in the hotels that proliferated near the rail depot, or chefs in the restaurants. These were the highest-paid blacks in the area.

6.

The 1940s were years of strife for the textile mills. Workers in the mills formed union locals and called strikes that crippled some of the mills, forcing some of the owners to sell and others to shut down. The new mill owners were absentee owners for the most part, and they cut their expenses by shutting down the company stores, paying in cash rather than by the "dookie books," and selling the mill houses and the water and sewer systems that served them. Workers who had rented their homes all their lives on easy terms found themselves queuing up at the bank to make monthly house payments; suddenly, too, they had property taxes and utility bills to pay.

The emigration of blacks from the county, which had begun after World

War I, took on added steam after World War II, as families moved to the North and to metropolitan areas in North Carolina to take advantage of a larger job market and — they hoped — more amicable race relations. But the black exodus didn't do much to improve the situation of the black families that remained, because the Richmond County job market was shrinking. By the 1970s, blacks formed less than one-fourth of the population of Richmond County, and most black families still lived in poverty.

Exceptions to the rule were black railroad workers and a few black professionals — teachers and school administrators in the "separate but equal" black school systems of the time, ministers, a handful of doctors and lawyers — and funeral home operators.

7.

Maceo's father, whose name was Maceo D. McEachern, grew up in neighboring Moore County — in Taylortown, a small unincorporated town (later incorporated) adjacent to the popular resort and golf community of Pinehurst. The first residents of Taylortown, early in the twentieth century, were all blacks: caddies on the Pinehurst golf courses and domestic employees at The Carolina Hotel, which — like the golf courses and, indeed, everything in the privately owned village of Pinehurst — was owned by the Tufts family. Visitors to Pinehurst were white, wealthy people of leisure from the North; later, many retired to the area to spend most of the year playing golf and riding to hounds. Annie Oakley retired from Buffalo Bill's Wild West Show to Pinehurst, where she gave shooting exhibitions at The Carolina to publicize the resort's skeet-shooting and trap-shooting facilities

The elder Maceo did not stay in Taylortown long after reaching adulthood. He made his way to Hamlet, seeing an opportunity to capitalize on the greater wealth of the town's black residents. He attended mortuary school, obtained his mortician's license, and started McEachern Funeral Home, which immediately got most of the "colored" funeral business from throughout Richmond County. The business was operating profitably by the early 1940s.

Prior to leaving Moore County, Maceo D. McEachern had married Vela Delois Raines. Vela had grown up in the tobacco-manufacturing city of Winston-Salem, about 70 miles north of Hamlet, graduated from Winston-Salem State Normal School (later Winston-Salem State University) and began a career as a public-school teacher. After 20 years as a teacher, Vela was to retire and become a licensed funeral director in order to help her husband in his business. Her last teaching job was in a one-room segregated school, where she taught six grades. "We used to go by that school in the school bus," said Pat Byrd, a white man who grew up in a rural area east of Hamlet and retired to the area years later, "and see Mrs. McEachern with those six classes of children in that little unpainted school with the woodstove for heat, and we knew that what we were hearing about 'separate or equal' schools was all bunk. But we were products of our society, and we just didn't give the matter that much thought."

Marrying Vela was a feather in Maceo's cap: She was a professional woman, and she had very light skin — and marrying a light-skinned woman was a definite signal of upward mobility for a black man in the 1930s. Somewhere in the Raines family's past, possibly as a result of forced miscegenation during slavery days, there was white blood — and also, Vela claimed, Native American blood. In later years, the younger Maceo, who was light-skinned like his mother, told of a couple of aunts who had "passed for white," merging into the predominantly white culture of the Winston-Salem area. (The story may have been apocryphal: "If there were such aunts," Naomi Daggs said, "they had to have been in a generation previous to Mrs. McEachern. She had only two sisters, and neither of them tried to pass for white.")

During their early years in Hamlet, Vela and the elder Maceo lived in a rooming house run by a black woman. They lived conventional lives, adapting themselves to the lower social status of blacks in Hamlet even though their educational and economic status was higher than that of many whites. But when it came time for them to build a home of their own, Maceo was determined to push the envelope of racial separatism: He bought a lot at the end of the black section of Charlotte Street — "the last lot before the white houses started," their son was to describe it — and built a two-story brick home with awnings and dormer windows.

Blacks in Hamlet simply did not live in brick houses in those years — and especially not in brick houses that abutted white neighborhoods. Time after time, local banks — whose officers and boards of directors were all white — turned down the McEacherns' application for a mortgage loan. They finally had to borrow the money in Winston-Salem, putting up the funeral home as collateral.

Once retired from teaching, Vela entered the funeral business enthusiastically, working alongside her husband. Preparing dead bodies for burial didn't seem to bother her at all. She was more practical than her husband, better at handling money, and she had a mercenary streak. The combination made her a formidable businesswoman, and the McEachern Funeral Home flourished.

Vela demonstrated her toughness and shrewdness in an episode that began with a young black man and woman showing up on her doorstep. The story they told her was bizarre and somewhat shocking. The man had raped the woman, but the woman had agreed not to press charges against him if he paid her an amount of money. The man agreed to pay the money, but to protect himself, he told her, he wanted the agreement in writing — and he wanted the agreement to be witnessed by a notary public, someone licensed by the State of North Carolina to witness deeds and contracts. They asked Vela to witness the agreement.

Vela read over the agreement, affixed her notary seal and signature to it, and made a copy — "for my records," she told them. She showed the two to the door and bade them farewell.

Then, still holding her copy of the incriminating document, she picked up her telephone and called the police.

8.

Vela always claimed to have been born in 1909, but family members said she had been born in 1907. She was 39 when her only child, Maceo Raines McEachern, was born on Nov. 6, 1946, and she doted on her son.

Vela was always a model of proper etiquette, and if she had controversial views on anything, she kept them to herself. She worried constantly that blacks, perceiving some slight or snub or *faux pas* in her, would take their business to another funeral home — or that whites, taking offense at some impolite or "uppity" action by her, would exert more subtle economic pressures on the business. From his earliest childhood, she instructed the younger Maceo in his behavior and insisted that he be polite and "get along" with everyone.

That wasn't a big order for Maceo, who cultivated his natural charm and playfulness and made friends with everybody he met, talking with the men on their own terms, flirting with the black women, treating white women like fragile ornaments. Growing up as he did between black and white neighborhoods, he associated with black children and white children alike — making a special friend of Lowery Ballard, the white boy who lived next door, but also playing with the poor black children from the "lower end" of Charlotte Street.

He got an early introduction to the arena of male camaraderie. Maceo D. McEachern was, as the vernacular description said, "bad to drink," and Vela would send the younger Maceo with him when he left the house, figuring that the boy's presence would keep the elder Maceo out of Hamlet's taverns and "juke joints." Vela never wised up to the fact that her ploy didn't work: Maceo D. simply took his son into the taverns with him. The younger Maceo never became much of a drinker, but he felt as comfortable in the taverns as he did in the women's parlors where the bodies of funeral-home clients were often laid out for viewing the night before a funeral.

It was as if Maceo had been born into two worlds, and had to learn to make his way in both. That tightrope act made him successful in business, romance, and politics, but it also created in him a desperate desire for attention and affection and made for deep schisms between the inner and outer man. To the end of his life, Maceo would always wonder if he made friends easily because people genuinely liked him, or if the easy friendships came about because his family had money and social standing.

III.

APRIL 13-18, 1991

1.

On the morning of April 13, 1991, after locking the concrete block he had found in Vela McEachern's driveway securely in the evidence vault at the police station, Chief Terry Moore got a call from a Charlotte attorney.

"He was hot to come down here and bring us a lot of documents," Moore said. "The documents had to do with the sports drink lawsuit, and I thought his calling us was ironic — because, even before we had left the crime scene the night before, some of the neighbors and friends of Maceo's who were hanging around had told us that they thought the murders had to do with this sports drink business. And Monte Irvin of Charlotte, who was involved in the drink's distribution, had already called me and tipped me off that there had been a lot of animosity over that drink.

"We thought ourselves that it was a good possibility that the murders stemmed somehow from the drink distribution deal. There's a saying that police have — 'Follow the money.' It means, when there's a murder, you look for whoever stands to profit financially from the death."

The attorney, who was representing Caldwell, brought Moore a huge sheaf of documents — copies of documents that had been filed with the court in Charlotte, in connection with Caldwell's suit against Clyde Sullivan.

In 1989, Caldwell, a body-builder and a former state karate champion, had invented Pro-Formance, a "high-energy drink" made with triple-filtered water from a North Carolina mountain spring, complex carbohydrates and potassium. The drink was designed to be ingested before workouts, to provide strength and endurance. Caldwell targeted fitness enthusiasts and the military as his top markets. He hired a marketer in June 1989, and a month later 500 fitness centers and gymnasiums in the Carolinas, Tennessee, Georgia, West Virginia and Florida were selling the drink.

Caldwell decided that, rather than paying a marketer to distribute the drink for him, he should sell the distribution rights for cash to pay his ever-mounting debts.

The lawsuit, which was filed in late January of 1991, alleged that Clyde Sullivan and his wife, Barbara Sullivan, plotted with Maceo McEachern and others to wrest control of the Charlotte company Gymbags Inc., which was doing business as Pro-Formance, from Caldwell and his wife, Barbara "Bobbie" Caldwell, the majority owners. It alleged that the Sullivans refused to take distribution orders for the drink, putting pressure on Gymbags' cash flow; and that they convinced Gymbags' banks to freeze the company's accounts, based on a false allegation that the Caldwells planned to withdraw the money and flee, leaving creditors in their wake.

The Caldwells fended off the Sullivans' improper pressure to sell, according to the suit. And when Maceo jumped from the Sullivans' side and made his own offer for the Pro-Formance name and trademark — not just the distribution rights — the Caldwells accepted his offer.

The attorney told reporters that Maceo would have been his strongest witness in court. "He was a particularly persuasive witness," the man said.

The attorney said Maceo split from the Sullivans because he saw that he could make a profitable deal himself — and because he feared a future clash with Clyde Sullivan.

After Caldwell's suit was filed, Sullivan's company sued Gymbags for breach of contract. Sullivan's attorney petitioned the court to dismiss the Caldwells' suit for lack of proper jurisdiction and other grounds. A hearing on that motion had been scheduled for April 30, 1991.

"This information made Clyde Sullivan a prime suspect in the murders," Moore said.

It did not escape the notice of investigators that Maceo had been shot in the mouth — a practice that had the weight of tradition. Supposedly, Mafia hit men always executed unfriendly witnesses by shooting them in the mouth.

"But it was also suspicious to us," said Moore, "that Joey Caldwell was so eager to get the information to us that he'd send his attorney to Hamlet just a few hours after the killings. In fact, we wondered how he had learned about the killings that quickly. The murders had been on the morning newscasts, but it must have taken a good bit of time to compile all those documents and make copies."

(Moore learned later that Drew Carver, an employee of Maceo's in Ventures, Inc., had telephoned Caldwell's house about 2:30 a.m. with the news.)

"The visit from the attorney made Joey Caldwell a prime suspect, too," Moore said, "especially after we learned that one of the clauses in the contract between Maceo and the Caldwells was that Maceo had to take out $2 million in 'key man' life insurance, to assure that the Caldwells would be paid for the distribution rights if something happened to Maceo.

"The key man insurance policies kicked in just a few days before the McEacherns were murdered.

"And the Caldwells, who had financial troubles and owed back taxes to the IRS, were the beneficiaries."

2.

"On alternate days," admitted Moore, "I would be convinced that Sullivan had hired somebody to kill Maceo, and that the hit man had killed Maceo's mother just to eliminate the only witness.

"But then, the next day, I would be equally convinced that Joey Caldwell had done it."

Other police officers and State Bureau of Investigation agents who were involved in the long investigation of the crime expressed similar uncertainty. All were virtually certain that either Caldwell or Sullivan was the killer — but they could not decide which.

For Naomi, Sullivan was the chief suspect. "I thought he was capable of hiring somebody to kill Maceo and his mother," she said. "The thought that Caldwell might have done it hardly crossed my mind. I had met Caldwell, and I could tell that he wasn't the sharpest knife in the case. I didn't think he had the intelligence to carry out a scheme like that and get away with it, leaving no clues. My other suspect, frankly, was a local businessman who had invested in Maceo's company, Ventures, Inc. I wondered for a long time if maybe he didn't have a part in the murders. I was willing to see anybody as a suspect."

Throughout the aftermath of the murders and the lengthy police investigation, Clyde Sullivan refused all requests by the press for interviews.

He was almost as cagey with police. He spoke three times with SBI agents, but never without an attorney's being present. They asked him to take a polygraph ("lie detector") test. He refused.

The Greensboro attorney who was representing Sullivan spoke once with a reporter, prior to Sullivan's first interview with the SBI. "Mr. Sullivan told me that he liked Maceo," he said. "He was very upset about it."

A few days after the McEachern murders, Moore got a call from Pat Reese, a veteran crime reporter for the Fayetteville Observer-Times in Fayetteville, some 55 miles to the northeast. Sullivan had major beer distribution facilities in Fayetteville, and Reese, too, had heard some of the stories about Sullivan's hard business dealings and volatile temper. He told Moore what he knew about Sullivan.

"What Reese told me made me even more suspicious of Sullivan," Moore admitted.

"You couldn't read all those depositions, and hear everything that had been said about Sullivan, and not believe that we had to resolve some issues with him. I met with Sullivan and his attorney. I told him, 'I understand you don't want to take a polygraph test. However, if a friend of mine had been killed, and I thought it might be of some benefit, however the inconvenience, I would do it.' The attorney told me, 'We'll let you know.' And that's where it stood, throughout the remainder of the investigation.

"Caldwell took the position that he had already had one (a polygraph test) done on his own, and that was that. But if he had done it, we were never privileged to see the results."

For his own part, Sullivan felt comfortable with the progress of the investigation. He had an unshakable alibi for the night of the killings. Sullivan had been at a party in a Moore County restaurant, twenty-five miles from Hamlet, surrounded for hours by dozens of people who could testify that he never left the room — certainly not for long enough to drive to Hamlet, kill the McEacherns, and drive back to the party.

Still, some investigators suspected that he had hired someone to carry out the killings.

Others — particularly SBI Special Agent Bill Lane, who, along with Special Agent Leroy Allen, were eventually assigned by SBI Director Charles Dunn full-time to the case for as long as it took to solve — concentrated on the possibility that Caldwell was the murderer.

"Mr. Lane had a vendetta against Joey Caldwell," Caldwell's cousin Bobby Peoples Jr. said later.

Lane maintained that he, too, "flip-flopped" in his opinions about the murderer's identity.

But the possibility that it was Caldwell was never far from his and Allen's minds from the time they drove up to the Caldwells' house on the afternoon of April 13, 1991.

In the driveway sat a late-model dark green Acura Legend — the type of car that witnesses had seen the night before, parked by the McEacherns' driveway. Although most of the witnesses had described the car as a Honda, the two makes are almost indistinguishable from each other.

3.

Maceo and Vela were laid to rest in Lincoln Memorial Park in Hamlet on April 18, 1991, after a joint funeral service — one of the largest such services in the history of Richmond County.

The service was held in the auditorium of Fairview Heights Middle School in Hamlet, the county's largest auditorium, with more seating capacity than any church sanctuary in the county. Still, hundreds of people stood outside the school and heard eulogies by six ministers piped through a public-address system.

A seventh brief eulogy was to have been delivered by Prentice Taylor, chairman of the county Board of Commissioners and longtime friend of Maceo who was to die a few months later of a heart attack — brought on, some said, by grief for his old friend.

Before the service, Taylor corralled a friend and read him his eulogy from his notes, asking the man if he thought it appropriate.

"I picture Maceo," Taylor said, "in the pastures of heaven. There is a beat-up old pickup truck for him to drive, and horses for him to ride, and somewhere nearby there will be a motorcycle. The grass will be the greenest he has ever seen, and he will eventually be reunited with all the friends he made here on earth — and they are legion."

The friend told Taylor that he thought Taylor's words were a beautiful tribute.

When it came time for Taylor to say the words again during the service, however, he wasn't able to finish the words.

He was crying too hard. He broke down and had to be led off the stage.

Maceo and Vela McEachern
Photo from the collection of Naomi Daggs

IV.

MACEO

1.

Maceo was a good student. Tutored at home by his mother, a former school-teacher, he had few academic difficulties.

He also made a name for himself locally as an athlete at Hamlet's "colored" high school, Monroe Avenue School. He went on to play football at North Carolina Central University in Durham, where he majored in physical education with a minor in biology.

At college, he drove a blue Corvette — a gift from his parents on gradua-tion from high school — and was popular with his classmates, to whom he would frequently lend money, his car, even his clothes. Maceo dated many girls in Durham, and had semi-serious relationships with a couple of them. At least one of the relationships continued for several years after college.

After graduating from North Carolina Central in 1968, Maceo rode a friend's motorcycle to the Woodstock Festival in upstate New York, returning to Hamlet full of stories about the places he had seen and the people he had met. He told friends that someday he wanted to ride his motorcycle across the country, and even into Canada, stopping at points along the way to meet new people and make new friends.

Maceo had ambitions of teaching school for a few years and then starting his own business. The public schools of Richmond County had been quietly integrated while Maceo was away at college — the transition being eased by a sports-mad white citizenry, who realized that an influx of black athletes would make the local high school teams more competitive in football, bas-ketball, baseball and track. There were now black administrators in many of the schools, and Maceo would have had no problem getting a teaching job. But he chose to teach physical education and serve as recreation director at Cameron Morrison Training School in Richmond County, a prison-like in-stitution for delinquent boys in the countryside north of Hamlet. The training school had been named for Cameron Morrison, the late governor and Red Shirt leader who had been born and reared in Rockingham, and an overwhelming majority of its inmates, drawn from a wide area of the state, were black. Maceo had help getting the job from Halbert and Gracie Jackson, friends from the North Yard section (now called Dobbins Heights) north of Hamlet; the Jacksons served as "house parents" at the training school.

The job lasted only two years. After his father became ill in 1970, Maceo attended the Cincinnati (Ohio) School of Mortuary Science — paying his own way by working as a YMCA athletic director in Cincinnati — and earned certification as a licensed embalmer and funeral director. Then he came back to Hamlet to help in the family business. When the elder Maceo McEachern died in 1971, his son stayed on to help Vela run the funeral home. Soon, mother and son built a second funeral home in the county seat of Rockingham.

Maceo never liked the job. He hated the smell of embalming fluid, hated working with dead bodies, hated the irregular hours and hated wearing a suit and tie. He also was beginning to chafe at his mother's insistence that he bow and scrape to everyone. Maceo made friends easily and didn't hold grudges, but he felt ashamed and hypocritical when he played up to people he didn't like.

Some of his mother's other attitudes toward the business irritated him, too. She was constantly worrying about potential disasters, keeping Maceo and the other employees on edge. And once, when a murdered woman's family called on a competitor, Nelson Funeral Service, to handle the funeral service and burial, Vela went to the county jail to talk to the woman's husband. The man, awaiting trial for his wife's murder, still had the legal authority to decide what funeral home would be in charge of the arrangements. Vela had him sign a contract with McEachern Funeral Home. The incident was an example of a mercenary streak in Vela that Maceo despised.

The irony was that Maceo had a mercenary streak of his own. He felt he could not declare independence from his mother until he had a secure and sizable income that did not depend on the funeral business.

But Vela held the purse strings at the funeral home, and Maceo felt that she did not pay him enough; at his rate of income, he would never be free. He constantly sought other means of income. In Cincinnati, he had lived in an up-scale apartment in a high-rise building, enjoyed his athletic director's job, and made a host of friends — most of whom were white. He even had a white girl-friend in Cincinnati, with whom he still kept in touch even though he was developing romantic relationships — some relatively serious, some of limited duration — with a procession of black women at home. He felt that he was in love with the Cincinnati woman, and he dreamed of going back to Ohio, marrying the woman, and settling down in a public recreation job while he worked to establish some business enterprise.

Even though a majority of his close friends were white, and even though he moved comfortably in white social circles, Maceo had had enough experience of racial discrimination to believe that wealth was a great equalizer. He dreamed of being rich enough to live on his own terms, and the devil take the hindmost.

2.

Maceo's standing in the community, his intelligence, his ability to win the friendships of both blacks and whites, and his attractiveness to women of both races did not go unnoticed in Richmond County's black community. Since school integration, many black leaders felt, it was high time that a black person was elected to the county Board of Education. But with only 18 percent of the county's registered voters being black, any successful candidate would have to be a person who could exert a substantial "crossover appeal" to white voters.

Many black leaders felt that Maceo was that person. "Maceo doesn't seem to know he's black," one friend joked, "and nobody else notices." He was amenable to their overtures, since he felt that success in politics could help him in business.

His quest for a seat on the school board began with a meeting at the home of Frank Fisher, a Hamlet man who owned nursing homes. Among the others present at the meeting were brothers J.W. and Alan Mask, longtime administrators in the county's former black school system, and Halbert Jackson, who had helped Maceo get his job at Cameron Morrison Training School. Jackson was active in the Dobbins Heights Community Association and had political ambitions of his own: In 1986, when the Community Association was successful in its petition to the state for Dobbins Heights to be allowed to incorporate as a town, Jackson became its first mayor, and his wife, Gracie, was elected to the Town Council. In 1972, Jackson eventually became Maceo's campaign manager — helping, among other things, to smooth the way for Sheriff R.W. Goodman's support.

White newspaper editor Glenn Sumpter agreed that the school board needed at least one black member — and to him, Maceo was the ideal candidate in 1972 despite being only 25 years old.

"Maceo was the all-time 'acceptable black' to whites in Richmond County, and that made him the ideal forerunner to all the black candidates who have come later," Sumpter said. "He was so light-skinned that some whites didn't realize that he was black. And militancy was not really in his nature. He was not personally bitter or angry about racial things — in fact, although some of his humor could have a biting edge to it, I never remember him being really angry about anything, and I never saw

Newspaper Editor Glenn Sumpter of the Richmond County Daily Journal Photo by Hugh Fleming.

him lose his temper. In his years on the school board and as a county commissioner, he made very certain that he represented black people; he was very aware that they were under-represented. But he was effective because he represented all the people, was not militant at all, and didn't offend anyone.

"In that first campaign, for the school board seat, he ran a great media campaign — some of it, on my advice. The campaign had a sort of reverse theme, with the slogan 'Why not McEachern?,' which made some white people face up to their deepest attitudes about race. *The Daily Journal* supported Maceo to the extent that we never ran his picture with our campaign coverage, and he never ran his picture with his campaign ads.

"The rest of the campaign was basically door to door, and he won people over largely on his personal charm. He never had to deal with a whole lot of really nasty racist stuff in the campaign."

Maceo couldn't have won without the sheriff's support, Sumpter noted. "Goodman gave him a kind of quasi-support, because he was aware that Maceo's clout in Hamlet could help him."

To Sumpter, "Maceo was a great politician. He had a great deal of self-confidence, and he was not the least bit uncomfortable in a group of white guys with red ties and blue suits. But he was also very conscious of the situations where being black could give him a bit of an edge."

In years to come, everyone in Richmond County was to hear various versions of a story about Maceo's first political campaign. Maceo was fond of telling the story, about a visit to a white political leader in a rural community in northwestern Richmond County, thirty miles from Hamlet. Maceo introduced himself, gave the man his card, and sat in the man's living room talking politics. "I like your ideas," the man said. "I'm going to vote for you, and I hope a lot of other people do, too. You know, there's a nigger from down in Hamlet running for the school board, and we've got to stick together and keep him from winning." Maceo gulped hard and told the man, "We certainly don't want that. Just remember to vote for McEachern."

In some versions of the story, the white man referred to him as "a nigger named "Mc-KAY-han," and Maceo retorted by urging the man to vote for "Mc-EECH-urn."

Some people believed that Maceo made up the story as an icebreaker. But Naomi Daggs, who was more familiar than anyone else with his tendency to embroider and embellish incidents in the re-telling, said, "I suspect that if Maceo had made up the story, it would have been a longer story."

The nonpartisan election for Board of Education was held on Saturday, May 6, 1972, and the results showed what a brilliant campaign Maceo and his backers had run. There were 10 candidates — Maceo, eight white men, and a white woman — in the race for three seats, and voters could mark their ballots for three candidates at most. Many blacks cast 'single-shot' ballots, voting only for Maceo. When the results were in, Maceo was the top votegetter with 2,503 votes — 364 more than the second-place candidate.

He was the first black elected to public office in Richmond County in seventy-four years.

3.

Maceo took office in December of that year, and it was an opportune time for a black school board member to get things done.

Earlier in the year, the Board of Education had fired a white teacher because she allegedly had an affair with a former student. The teacher sued the board and hired black Charlotte attorney Julius Chambers to represent her. A Board of Education attorney paid a visit to Chambers' office and soon thereafter recommended that the board reinstate the teacher. "Even the lobby and corridors of Chambers' office are carpeted," the attorney said. His message was unmistakable: The Chambers firm had a lot of money and other resources, and it was known for representing blacks in civil rights cases.

The school board would have to take notice of blacks in the school system.

Many of the Richmond County school system's black employees were "non-certified personnel" — school bus mechanics, custodians, cafeteria workers, secretaries and clerks. A big percentage of these employees were so low-paid that they were eligible for food stamps. Maceo and his fellow school board member Jimmy Maske — a white man from Rockingham, and no relation to the black Hamlet school administrator J.W. Mask, also called "Jimmy" — pushed hard for the board to grant substantial increases in pay and benefits for these workers. They prevailed over early opposition from other board members.

Maceo had other successes as a member of the Board of Education. Here, as in other areas of his life, he was able to use his charm and intelligence to convince others that his opinions were right. Often, he used gentle humor to make his point.

Glenn Sumpter referred to Maceo as "the beige prince." And in Richmond County, it sometimes seemed that Maceo was the closest thing to royalty. Once, in fact, indulging his penchant for harmless practical jokes, he had impersonated a visiting "Jamaican prince," wearing a brightly colored headdress and a dashiki, during the opening moments of a school board social. Though he was a member of the board, no one there had recognized him until he took off the headdress.

School board members served six-year terms. During his six years on the board, Maceo branched out with business ventures and civic work, so that by 1978, he had a broad and complex network of relationships all over Richmond County and beyond.

4.

Jimmy Maske had won election to the Richmond County Board of Commissioners in 1976, resigning his seat on the school board. He urged Maceo to run for a seat on the Board of Commissioners in 1978. As a commissioner, Maceo could have a major influence on every aspect of county government, not just the schools.

The challenge appealed to Maceo. Assured of the sheriff's support, though Goodman's support was lukewarm, he tossed his hat into the ring.

Richmond County commissioners were elected under a district system, usually for four-year terms. But Prentice Taylor was running for the district seat in Marks Creek Township, where Maceo lived. Taylor was a friend of Maceo's, a man whose opinions Maceo respected, and even if Maceo were to run against him in the May Democratic primary election, the popular Taylor would be a formidable — probably unbeatable — opponent. Maceo decided to run for an "at-large" seat. If he won, he would be required to run for re-election at two-year intervals.

Only a plurality of the vote was required to win nomination in the May Second Democratic primary. The presence of six white men in the race virtually assured Maceo's victory, since they would divide much of the white vote among them while blacks would cast single-shot ballots for Maceo. He won the nomination with 2,612 votes — just 30.3 percent of the total vote cast, but 567 more than the candidate who finished second. On November 7, he easily won the election over the Republican candidate, 4,995 votes to 3,103. Party was more important than race to most of Richmond County's Democrats, who numbered more than 75 percent of registered voters.

Prentice Taylor easily won election to his four-year seat, giving Maceo and Maske another important ally on the board.

In his first two-year term, Maceo alienated the sheriff, who believed that the commissioners he had supported for election should vote as he instructed them to vote. Goodman found that Maceo was his own man.

In the May 6, 1980, Democratic primary, therefore, Maceo found himself running against one of Goodman's oldest and closest political allies, who had previously served several terms on the Board of Commissioners before losing the 1974 Democratic primary to Vernon McDonald, a political maverick who was not beholden to Goodman and who became a close ally and friend to Maceo. It figured to be Maceo's toughest campaign to date.

Maceo won the primary without the necessity of a runoff, garnering 3,576 votes to a total of 3,558 for his opponent and another white candidate. He coasted to a second two-year term without opposition in November.

By 1982, Goodman was determined to oust Maceo from office. This time, he persuaded another black man — Azriah Ellerbe, a Community Action adminis-trator — to run against Maceo. Also in the race was Doris Cannon, male despite his name, a white follower of the sheriff who had never before held public office. Goodman's strategy was for Maceo and Ellerbe to split the black vote, assuring Cannon's nomination.

In the June 29 primary, Maceo led the balloting with 2,313 votes — but the 1,249 votes for Ellerbe kept him from gaining a majority. He was forced into a July 27 second primary against Cannon. Things still looked good for Maceo, but Cannon (and Goodman) had counted on the traditional low turnout among blacks for a second primary, and they got it. Cannon won the second primary with 2,700 votes to Maceo's 2,190.

The results showed that race was still a factor in Richmond County poli-tics — because, in the same July 27 primary, Vernon McDonald had won a narrow victory in spite of the sheriff's best efforts.

5.

Maceo considered his four years as a county commissioner a success. They were years of progress for Richmond County and its citizens. Leading the way on the Board of Commissioners, along with Maceo, were Maske, Vernon McDonald, Taylor (who later was to become chairman of the board), and Chairman Richard Conder. None of the five was a member of Goodman's local political machine.

The four years also made for a number of funny stories — some told by Maceo, others told about him. "Being funny just came naturally to Maceo," Glenn Sumpter said. "He had as quick a wit as anybody I ever knew. He would never tell you a lot about his inner feelings, but he was capable of doing an entire impromptu standup comedy routine at a party, and sometimes you could gauge his feelings from the funny stories he told. His humor often had a bit of an edge to it."

At one meeting, a woman who lived at the edge of one school district asked the commissioners to allow her to drive her children to school in another district. She left for work before the school bus arrived, she explained, but her drive to work took her right past the school in the other district. She could drop the children off there and not have to pay a day-care center or be late for work. She had earlier asked the school board for the same consideration, but the board had refused to grant an exception to its rule that children must attend school in the district where they live. (The rule has since been relaxed.)

Conder, presiding at the meeting, explained to the woman that the district system was a matter of school board policy and the commissioners could do nothing to change it. "I'm sorry, but we can't help you," he said. He raised his gavel, ready to proceed to the next item on the agenda.

"This reminds me," Maceo broke in, "of the time many years ago when some people who lived in Cordova didn't want their children going to the Cordova School. They wanted them to go to the Rockingham Grammar School instead. The school in Rockingham was bigger, had a bigger library and more resources, and they considered it a better school."

"We need to move on, Maceo," Conder said.

Maceo seemed oblivious to Conder's entreaty. "These people kept sending their children to Cordova School, but finally another idea occurred to some of them. They got the idea of claiming that their children were being harmed psychologically in some way by going to school at Cordova while their friends were going to Rockingham, which had a gymnasium for them to play in and a big auditorium to give plays in."

"Maceo —" Conder said.

"So they got the idea," Maceo went on, "of taking their children to their family doctors and getting the doctors to sign a statement that being forced to go to Cordova School was harming their children psychologically. Now, a lot of these people had been going to the same doctors for years, and taking their children to them, and even if the statements they were asking the doctors to sign were little white lies, that was all right with most of the doctors, because they were helping out the families and it didn't really go against the Hippocratic Oath to tell a little white lie on behalf of a patient."

Conder, finally realizing where Maceo was going with his extended story, laid down his gavel. He knew that people in Cordova were fiercely proud of the academic reputation of their little community school, and that Maceo was making the whole thing up.

"And so," Maceo, obviously enjoying himself, said, "the families took their children to the doctors, and got the doctors to sign statements that the children were being harmed psychologically but that everything would be all right if they could just be allowed to go to Rockingham Grammar School, and then they took those statements to the school board, and the school board allowed it.

"Most doctors in those days, you see, were willing to oblige their patients that little bit. I imagine a lot of doctors even today would oblige their patients the same way, if they could.

"Well, my story doesn't really have a point. I just wanted to talk a little bit about something I remembered. I'm really sorry we can't help you, ma'am."

The other commissioners had trouble concealing smiles at Maceo's story without a point.

A fringe benefit of being a county commissioner was the annual junket to the weeklong National Association of Counties convention (Conder was later to become president of the national organization). Maceo was fond of telling about one such trip, when he and Vernon McDonald played the slot machines at Las Vegas early one evening and Vernon won $250.

"Dinner's on me, Maceo," Vernon said.

They found an upscale restaurant on the Strip, and the waiter came to take their order. McDonald ordered dinner, then said, "and bring us the most expensive bottle of wine you've got."

When the bill came, McDonald's eyes almost popped out of his head. "Eight hundred dollars for a bottle of wine!" he almost shouted as he thumbed through his credit cards.

"Well, Vernon, you did say you wanted the most expensive bottle they had," Maceo reminded him.

"Yeah, but in Richmond County, that'd be sixteen dollars," McDonald said.

Sometimes, Maceo's humor had a sharp racial edge. At a National Association of Counties convention in Chicago, Maceo and Prentice Taylor stepped onto a chartered bus together and Maceo took a seat near the front. "Boy," roared Taylor, "don't you know your place? Your kind belongs at the back of the bus!"

Maceo tugged at his forelock, stood up, bowed from the waist and said, "Yassuh, Boss. I'm sorry, Boss," and trudged to the back of the bus.

Several conventioneers from Northern states approached Maceo the next day to commiserate and tell him how embarrassed for him they had been. That it was all a rather crude joke became apparent only that night, when the two entered the bus again and Taylor took a seat near the front. "Boy," Maceo told him, "don't you know your place?…"

Not everyone appreciated that sort of rough-edged humor, but people who knew Maceo had to get used to it.

6.

Maceo did not totally regret being out of public office for the first time in ten years. His business and community obligations were taking bigger and bigger bites of his time.

He was a trustee of St. Stephens A.M.E. Zion Church in Hamlet. He was a director of Richmond Memorial Hospital in Rockingham. He was a director of First Scotland Bank in Rockingham, and he was a member of the Richmond Industrial Team, which worked to recruit new and larger industries to the county. He was vice president of the Rockingham Jaycees. In many of these organizations, he was the first and/or only black.

He was a director of McLaurin Center, a "sheltered workshop" in Hamlet where mentally handicapped adults learned trades and earned independent incomes by manufacturing various simple products, mostly of wood, on contracts with area businesses.

"Maceo was a kind of patron saint of the mentally handicapped in Hamlet," Naomi Daggs said. She recalled one man in particular, a victim of microcephaly who would stand in his family's front yard in East Hamlet when the weather was good and wave to motorists passing by on Highway 74. "Anytime he started to drive somewhere and had the time," she said, "he would drive by there so he could wave back to the man."

Maceo's charitable work included many private gestures that he kept secret. Mildred Stanback, an elderly woman in Hamlet who had limited education, depended on Maceo to take her to the grocery store, pay bills, help her complete written forms or business correspondence, and — on at least one occasion — counsel her headstrong young nephew.

He also served as an unofficial guardian to an elderly invalid man. "Maceo ran errands, paid his bills, had his prescriptions filled, and dropped by just to chat or check on the old gentleman," Naomi said. "I never knew what the old man's name was; Maceo and his mom simply referred to him as 'Maceo's little man.' "

7.

Still determined to break free of his mother's domination, Maceo had no lack of ideas for making money, and most proved successful to an extent.

He set up his own private corporation, Ventures, Inc., into which he channeled income from a variety of business interests. With a white friend, Mike

McInnis, he owned and bred quarter horses. The operation was called 4M Quarter Horses, taking its name from the alliterative initials of the two owners. He was president of another company, Pinehurst Development Corporation, which contracted with builders to erect residential tracts in Moore and Richmond Counties, the largest of which was McEachern Forest. Maceo also worked hard at an Amway dealership in the late 1980s and had some success, especially at nearby Fort Bragg, where he enlisted the aid of some black officers in getting Amway products placed in the post exchange.

In February 1991, after several similar ventures, he entered into a business arrangement that, he told friends, would enable him to achieve his dream. He signed a contract giving him trademark and distribution rights to a "sports drink" called Pro-Formance, which had been developed by Joey Caldwell.

V.

JOEY AND BOBBIE

1.

Joey Dean Caldwell promised his wife Bobbie Caldwell that he would be a millionaire before his 35th birthday.

He just made it — but at age 37, he was broke and in debt again.

It was just the latest chapter in an up-and-down life that started in a working-class home. Joey, born on June 20, 1956, was the oldest of three children of Floy Dean Caldwell and Joyce Caldwell, and the only son. The family moved often, because Floy Dean was in the U.S. Air Force.

"Only a mama could love that man," one acquaintance of Joey Caldwell remarked of him. And Joyce Caldwell, only 16 at the time of Joey's birth, indeed lavished love on her firstborn.

Loving him must have been difficult. From an early age, he ate most of his meals in his room, refusing to eat with the family. He avoided family outings whenever possible. Years later, his mother said Joey "did not have close relations with anybody."

He did his own laundry, because he was a stickler for neatness and cleanliness and didn't want his clothing "mixed" with that of his parents and sisters. Besides, he said, his mother didn't fold his clothes right.

The Caldwells divorced, and Joey went with his mother to Keystone, Florida. But when he was about to enter high school, he returned to live with his father in Gastonia, without explaining why. Years later, he told his mother that Keystone was too small for him to make anything of himself there.

Besides, a girl in Keystone had made fun of him.

Girls had become important to Joey. He quit high school at age 17 to get married and take a job as a used-car salesman. Later, he learned tool-and-die making. It was a good working-class living, but Joey yearned for wealth, fame and power.

2.

That first marriage didn't last long. It was to be the first of four marriages.

Joey, like Clyde Sullivan, had a reputation for violent outbursts of temper, and his outbursts tended to frighten his wives and drive them away. And like Sullivan, he had once been charged with assault — only, in his case, the assault had been made with a gun.

Once, when the ex-husband of Joey's second wife arrived to take custody of his son for a weekend, Joey fired a handgun into the side of the man's car.

No one was hurt — and, as in the assault case involving Sullivan, the parties settled out of court and the charge was dropped.

A neighbor testified in court in 1993 that Joey had gone into an almost uncontrollable rage over the presence of the family dogs in the house as he and his fourth wife, Bobbie, were getting ready to entertain guests.

And Bobbie once told a friend that she considered that her chief duty as Joey's wife was "to keep Joey from getting angry."

3.

Associated Press picture of Joey Caldwell. Photo by Clark Cox. Clipping from the collection of Naomi Daggs.

Joey achieved a measure of local fame through bodybuilding. He started working out in gyms and took steroids. He won bodybuilding competitions and state titles in karate in 1976 and 1977. By 1991 he was a compact, heavily muscled man, five feet seven inches tall, weighing 195 pounds, with a tanning-booth tan and a brusque, in-your-face manner.

He made his first foray into business in 1985, founding Vitamin Locker with financial help from his third wife. Vitamin Locker was a 12-employee company that ordered bodybuilding supplements — calcium, liver pills, amino acids — from New York, bottled them with its own labels, advertised widely and took orders by telephone from workout gyms and fitness centers across the country.

Joey divorced his third wife, and soon thereafter he met Bobbie Burford Riggins in a Charlotte gym and began dating her. Bobbie was the daughter of a Virginia pharmaceutical salesman and had been married from 1981 to 1985 to Randy Riggins, a Charlotte man who now worked as an insurance agent and wrote some of the Caldwells' insurance policies.

Joey began dating Bobbie in 1987, and in June of that year he moved into her house in Charlotte. Later that summer, he asked her for a loan to pay for advertising for Vitamin Locker in some national magazines. She lent him $25,000, which she borrowed by using as collateral stock that she had inherited from her father. Joey never paid back the loan, and she eventually had to sell the stock to pay off the loan she had taken out.

Still, Bobbie, who had been a schoolteacher, went to work at Vitamin Locker in October 1987, as office manager and telemarketer, and she married Joey on Aug. 20, 1988. "From that point on," she said, "we spent all of the time together. We worked together, we ate together, we went to the gym together, and we slept together."

Joey and Bobbie started another company, Active Woman, featuring a women's line of bodybuilding nutritional supplements. Investors in that company included Bobbie's ex-husband, Randy Riggins, and her mother, Martha Burford, who lived in Belmont. But Active Woman never really got off the ground.

Financial troubles struck the Caldwells from another side in late 1989, when two of Vitamin Locker's top salesmen left the company and struck out on their own, taking with them contacts they had made with gyms and fitness centers across the southeastern United States. Joey had incurred major debts in the course of operating Vitamin Locker and Active Woman, and he decided to try to recoup by founding another company, Gymbags. He incorporated the company in Bobbie's name as owner, so that it would not be liable for the debts he had personally guaranteed for Vitamin Locker and Active Woman. But he held the title of president of the company, and employees of the company and such contract workers as attorneys and accountants took their orders from him. Bobbie remained office manager.

Gymbags, Bobbie later recalled, "was a line of clothing that we started — clothing, pants, and that sort of thing — that you could wear in the gym, and we never did much with that. But we started the drink Pro-Formance in that company."

Joey wanted to develop a sports drink that was not sodium-based and that was high in complex carbohydrates to provide energy. He took his idea to a chemist in Greensboro, and they worked on the formulation in February and March of 1990.

Joey approached Nathan and Carolyn Arthur, who ran Arcadia Farms, an independent bottling company in the western North Carolina town of Arden, with something he called "Pro Power." The drink was modeled after Gatorade, the leader in the sports-drink market — but unlike Gatorade, Pro Power was low in sodium and was meant to be drunk before, not after, workouts, in order to provide quick energy and stamina.

The idea was dynamite, the Arthurs agreed. But the drink looked cloudy in the bottle, it was too sweet, and it spoiled if left on the shelf too long.

The Arthurs brought their expertise to the formula. Working together, Joey and the Arthurs finally came up with Pro-Formance. The drink looked like a winner and caught the interest of marketers throughout the booming physical fitness field.

Buoyed more by the idea of all the wealth that would soon be coming to them than by any real money, the Caldwells began to live in high style. They bought a $140,000 home — relatively expensive, for Gaston County — in the upscale Forest Cove development near Belmont, furnished it with the best furniture they could buy on credit, and began to take all their meals at restaurants unless they were entertaining guests. They had no children, but they treated their two cocker spaniels almost like children, taking them regularly to expensive grooming salons. Bobbie bought a huge and impressive collection of "collector plates," which she displayed in a custom-made glass cabinet just off the foyer of the house.

"The house looked like one of those 'show homes,' not like a house that somebody actually lived in," Hamlet police officer Jim Thomas said.

Joey dressed in tailored suits that cost $1,000 and more. He explained this extravagance by saying that his success in bodybuilding had made it impossible to fit him with off-the-rack suits.

In order to fuel this lavish lifestyle, the Caldwells had to make a success of Pro-Formance. They approached a Gastonia, North Carolina, man, Ben Rudisill, about marketing the drink through his company Rudisill Enterprises, and he succeeded in placing it widely at gyms and fitness centers across the Southeast. Through the Arthurs, Joey also met Maceo McEachern and contracted with him to sell Pro-Formance to the military outlets at Fort Bragg. In late 1990, Joey went with Rudisill to a beer wholesalers' convention in Tennessee, and Joey convinced several of those wholesalers to start distributing Pro-Formance in other areas of the country.

Joey also met Clyde Sullivan at the convention. He worked out an arrangement for Sullivan Wholesalers to sell Pro-Formance in the Southern Pines and Fayetteville areas.

Pro-Formance, with more than a dozen distributors throughout the United States, was bringing in money for the Caldwells, but Joey wanted more. He decided to try to find a buyer for the Pro-Formance formula and trademark, and Sullivan was interested.

"We decided," Bobbie said, "to sign a contract with Sullivan — not with Sullivan Wholesalers, but with Clyde Sullivan. He developed a company called Pro-Formance International, where they were going to be a master distributor for the company. And they would set up distributors all over the United States for the product."

Sullivan and the Caldwells signed the contract establishing Pro-Formance International on Halloween night of 1990.

At the time, the Caldwells didn't realize that Sullivan knew a great deal about their business problems. Joey and several area distributors of Pro-Formance had attended a meeting earlier that month at Sullivan's home, to work out details of the distribution agreement with Pro-Formance International. When Joey departed, he left his briefcase behind, not missing it until he had driven past Pinebluff, several miles down U.S. Highway 1. He telephoned Sullivan from his car phone, telling him he would come back and get the briefcase — and, according to what Sullivan later told acquaintances, expressing some anger that Sullivan had let him walk away without the briefcase. Joey retrieved the briefcase, but not before Sullivan had worried open its combination lock and read over the balance sheets inside. He realized that the Caldwells were skating along the edge of financial disaster.

Joey didn't know that Sullivan had read his balance sheets until Maceo told him about it the next January.

Sullivan used his knowledge of the Caldwells' cash-flow problems to put the squeeze on them. He ordered two shipments of Pro-Formance for his own wholesaling company to distribute, but he refused to accept orders for the product from other distributors.

"It stopped (our) cash flow," Bobbie said, "and it was — it was a very stressful situation. We had no cash flow, and we had obligated debts for the company, so (Joey) was very upset and under a tremendous amount of stress."

The stress manifested itself in disturbing ways. Throughout their marriage, Bobbie said, Joey had been an occasional sleepwalker. But now, the sleepwalking was combined with near-violent actions that scared Bobbie.

"He slept with a gun in the nightstand, right next to him," Bobbie said, "and he would — he would grab the gun out of the nightstand and point it at the walls and start screaming and hollering that somebody was breaking into the house." Once, she said, "There were shadows on the (bedroom) wall on my left side, and he reached into the nightstand, rolled onto the floor next to the bed, crouching over the bed, cocked the gun, and pointed it over the top of me, pointing it at the wall. ... I jumped out of the bed and ran behind him and told him no one was there. And then he stood up and walked into the bathroom, and when he came out of the bathroom, he had uncocked the gun and was awake."

During the sleepwalking episodes, Bobbie said, "He would think that somebody was breaking into the house per Clyde Sullivan's instructions."

Joey's suspicions of Sullivan grew deeper after an incident that Bobbie recalled as taking place on "the 18th or 19th of December" 1990. Sullivan, she said, came to the Caldwells' office in Charlotte. "I was walking out of the elevator door at the time he was walking in, so I got back on the elevator and asked him why he was coming. He was very belligerent and very threatening to me. He said, 'You know why I am here. (It) is to stop you all from stealing money out of the company.'...

"When we walked into the office, he came up with two armed guards — two deputy sheriffs from his county ... and Maceo was there. And when we walked into the office ... he pushed me away, and he stormed back to Joey's office and Joey met him at the door. ... Then they had this confrontation in the office."

Bobbie did not hear the conversation between Joey and Sullivan, but Joey later told her that Sullivan had threatened him. What Maceo later told Richmond County Sheriff R.W. Goodman confirmed Joey's account of the confrontation.

Still, negotiations to sell all rights to Pro-Formance, including the trademark and formula, plowed ahead during December and January, with Sullivan as the prospective buyer. Sullivan had the Caldwells over a barrel financially, but he also had money and badly wanted all rights to the popular drink.

Lawyers working with Gymbags during the negotiations brought up the subject of key man insurance. That, Bobbie said, was when Joey "started talking about a plan to kill Clyde Sullivan, after he had purchased the company, after the insurance was in place."

Bobbie agreed to help out by providing Joey with an alibi.

The Caldwells were not able to work out an agreement with Sullivan — his offer was not as much as they needed to resolve their debts — so they began talking with Maceo about buying the Pro-Formance formula and trademark.

They also began talking to each other about plans to kill Maceo.

4.

In late 1990, the Caldwells took a weekend trip to Myrtle Beach, South Carolina, a popular weekend getaway for Carolinians. There, Joey spotted a car with an Ontario license plate in a parking lot. He unscrewed the plate and threw it into the trunk of his own BMW. On the way back from the beach, they drove by the McEachern home, and Joey took photographs of the house and yard to familiarize himself with the layout.

On January 17, 1991, the Caldwells left Belmont for a visit to Joey's mother in Starke, Florida. On the way back from that visit, on January 21, they stopped at Mac's Gun Shop in Garden City, Georgia, on the outskirts of Savannah, and Joey bought a double-barreled shotgun with an unusual over-and-under barrel conformation and a box of ammunition for it. He filled out the "Firearms Transaction Form" required by the state of Georgia as "Arthur Scott," listing an address in Browning, West Virginia. There was an uneasy moment when it developed that another couple in the store actually lived in West Virginia and wanted to talk about their home state with Joey. But he got through the conversation without blowing his cover.

Joey bought oversized camouflage clothing, boots, and a hat to wear when he went to Hamlet to murder Maceo. And, Bobbie said, he made plans to disguise his wife's Acura automobile, which he planned to drive to Hamlet: "He bought some metallic kind of tape to go down the sides of the car, to make it look like it had been painted on the sides. And he had bought … just plain brown tape to cover up the emblems on the car so that it wouldn't look like it was an Acura."

Bobbie said that Joey told her that he would "drill out" the serial number of the shotgun so that it could not be traced to him if it were ever recovered by lawmen. She said she never saw him working on the shotgun, but shortly after the conversation, she did hear him working in their garage with a drill.

5.

Maceo, through his company Ventures, Inc., bought Pro-Formance on February 15, 1991. The sale price was $235,000, with $40,000 to be paid at the time of the sale, $20,000 in December of 1991, and three additional lump-sum yearly payments. Maceo agreed to take out $1 million in key man life insurance, supposedly to guarantee payment to the Caldwells in case of his death. He was uncomfortable about the face value of the insurance policy, which was more than four times the sale price. The $1 million, they assured him, was based on estimated royalty proceeds to the Caldwells from a five-year marketing plan, which stipulated that the Caldwells would receive 3 cents for every gallon sold of Pro-Formance.

But $1 million would hardly have been enough to get the Caldwells out of debt. They decided, without telling Maceo, to increase the value of the life insurance to $2 million.

The Caldwells, with Randy Riggins as their major advisor, agreed to help Maceo shop for the lowest premiums for the life insurance. No insurer would write insurance for the full amount, so they settled on a $1.5 million policy from Sun Life Assurance and a $500,000 policy from Great West Life Assurance.

Maceo showed an elevated blood-pressure reading in his initial physical examination for one of the policies. In court later, under questioning by a prosecuting attorney, Riggins recalled: "…I took a medical examiner with me to a meeting up at the office of Parker, Poe (the Caldwells' attorneys), in Charlotte, and had (Maceo's) blood pressure read."

Q. Did you get medical forms back from a Dr. Wendell Wells, if you recall?
A. I did.
Q. Did you — was there any delay, if you recall, at all in getting these medical forms back?

A. He was slow to respond.

Q. Was there any — what, if anything, did Joey and Bobby Caldwell say to you about that, if you recall?

A. They — I received numerous calls in an effort to expedite having the insurance issued from Bobby and Joey. And I indicated to them I was doing the best I could; that we had a hold-up with the physician in Hamlet, Maceo's doctor; and up until that information was received, I couldn't finish the case. So, between me and my secretary, we made numerous calls to Dr. Wells.

Q. As a result of the phone call from Bobby and Joey Caldwell?

A. Correct.

Q. Did you feel pressure from them to get this statement from Dr. Wells?

A. Well, they — well, yes, they were aggressive. I can remember asking Bobbie, you know, "What is the hurry?" And she said, "We just really want to get this business deal behind us, and move on with our life." So, finally, we got the information from Dr. Wells and proceeded.

Maceo signed the applications for the insurance policies — apparently not noticing that their face values had been increased, since he told acquaintances later that he had taken out $1 million in key man insurance and still felt uncomfortable about it.

Nothing in the policies stipulated that the insurance payoffs were to be tied to Maceo's debts to the Caldwells. Nor, according to later testimony in civil lawsuits against the insurance companies, did either Riggins or other representatives of the two insurance companies ever investigate, or know anything about, the five-year income projection, which was based on optimistic expectations of Pro-Formance's future sales rather than on the drink's sales record to date.

6.

Sometime in early April, Joey drove by a construction site in Charlotte and saw some concrete blocks lying in the dirt near the road. He stopped his car, picked up one of the blocks, and put it into the trunk of the car.

Bobbie Caldwell picked up a copy of the Great West policy at the insurance agent's office on April 4, and she picked up a copy of the Sun Life policy on Wednesday, April 10. The copies assured the Caldwells that both policies were in full effect.

Joey left for Hamlet later on April 10, to kill Maceo. Before he left, he wrote and mailed to himself a letter, showing it to Bobbie. The letter, she said, "state(d) that he completely lost it, and he was on a rampage; that he was going to kill anybody that was involved with the sale of the company, or putting us in a position where we had to sell the company. … He wrote that letter so that if something happened to him, and he was caught, that it would cover for me."

(Several days later, she said, when the letter arrived at the Gymbags post office box, Joey tore it up and burned the pieces.)

Joey drove to Hamlet. He had met with Maceo on earlier occasions in Vela's home, delivering vanloads of Pro-Formance to Maceo, and he was under the mistaken impression that Maceo, being unmarried, lived with his mother. He drove to Vela's home, parked his car along the street, lugged the concrete block to the center of the driveway and returned to his car to wait.

Vela was already home, but Maceo did not come to his mother's home that night.

After Joey returned home, Bobbie said, "I was upset over the fact of him going down there, and we discussed not doing that, and doing other things — doing something else, having another option. And we had pretty much agreed to just drop the whole issue and do something else financially, and then we went to bed."

After they awoke, however, according to Bobbie's account, "Joey made the statement that he was going to go back down there, and not come back until it was done."

VI.
MACEO AND NAOMI

1.

On a day in late summer 1972, shortly after Maceo's election to the Richmond County Board of Education, he was standing on the sidewalk outside Swails Shoe Shop in Hamlet, selling raffle tickets to benefit a project in one of the county's public schools.

He saw Gloria Fisher, wife of his political mentor Frank Fisher, enter the store with a young black woman he hadn't seen before; she was wearing hip-hugger jeans, and he couldn't help noticing — as he told her later — that she wore them well.

When the two came out of the store, Maceo was waiting. On the pretext of selling Gloria Fisher a raffle ticket, he managed an introduction to the other young woman. The woman was Gloria's cousin, who had moved to Hamlet only a week or so earlier.

Her name was Naomi Washington Daggs. She was to be Maceo's girlfriend for most of the last 19 years of his life.

2.

Naomi Washington, born in 1941, was five years older than Maceo. She grew up in a row house in Washington, D.C., the daughter and only child of federal civil servants. The house was also home to both her grandmothers and, from time to time, to an assortment of other family members and hangers-on. It was an unusual household, populated by unusual people.

Naomi's mother worked for the federal Bureau of Engraving in Washington, where she had been one of the first black employees; for several years after she started the job, her workplace still had separate restrooms for blacks and whites. She eventually lost the job after she took and passed a civil service examination for a friend, a housewife who was desperate to find a job so that she could escape an abusive husband and support her children. The friend also got a job at the Bureau of Engraving — but the friend's estranged husband learned about the exam fraud and turned both women in. They were both fired, and both took jobs as cocktail waitresses in the Officers' Club at Boling Air Force Base.

"The tips were good, and they actually made more money as cocktail waitresses than they had made working for the government," Naomi recalled in early 2001. "My mother worked there for several years. But she didn't want to be a cocktail waitress for the rest of her life, so she went to cosmetology school and opened her own beauty shop."

In 2001, Naomi had recently moved to a house in a residential development south of Rockingham, which she shared with her 78-year-old mother. Her mother had been diagnosed with Alzheimer's Disease in 1989, and when her second husband died in 1990, responsibility for her care fell to Naomi and Naomi's aunt, who alternated keeping her in their homes. She moved in with Naomi for good in 1998.

Naomi's father, whose grandparents had been slaves on a farm adjacent to Thomas Jefferson's estate in Virginia, worked for the U.S. Department of Labor until his retirement. He functioned well at work, but he was an alcoholic. When he was on drinking binges, he squandered his family's money. Naomi's mother finally decided to separate from him, but he refused to leave the house. She left, but came back. During most of Naomi's growing-up years, her parents lived in the same house with her, but they occupied different areas of the house. Her father slept on the first floor, as did Naomi. Her mother lived upstairs, sharing a kitchenette with Naomi's grandmothers. The grandmothers got along fine with each other and with Naomi's mother.

But the grandmothers were an odd couple. Naomi's maternal grandmother had moved to Washington from Warrenton, Virginia, after her husband, Naomi's grandfather, died. "She was a soft-spoken woman who hummed all the time and did all the cooking," Naomi recalled. "She was the only one in the house who could cook well, because she wouldn't let anybody else cook." The grandmother had learned cooking and other domestic skills early in life. Her mother had abandoned the family, and her two older sisters had left home at age 13 or 14 to work as live-in domestics, leaving her, at age seven, the only female in a household with a father and five brothers.

Naomi's paternal grandmother was a feisty, outspoken woman who had made a good living as a bootlegger in the 1930s and early 1940s. "My grandfather was really proud — his parents had been 'house Negroes' in slavery times, and that was a matter for pride to some black people in those days — but he was basically a farm laborer," Naomi said. "Everybody wondered how he could afford his own house — even one he built himself — and 90 acres of land and two cars on a laborer's wages. It was because of the money my grandmother brought in, selling illegal whiskey." But this grandmother was asthmatic, and when her husband took a better-paying job on a large horse farm in The Plains, Virginia, she began to suffer from asthma attacks in the late summer and early autumn because their house was surrounded by hay fields. "She began to stay with us during haying season, and every year her visits lasted a little longer," Naomi said. "Finally, she stayed six or seven months a year."

There was a three-bedroom apartment in the basement of the Washington house. It seemed to Naomi that almost every member of her extended family who was out of work or needed assistance of whatever sort took up residence there for a while, as did some friends of the Washington family and relatives of friends.

"It was Family Central," she recalled. "Every major family event took place in our house. I've always been a 'people person,' fond of being around a lot of people, and I think it's because there were always a lot of people around when I was growing up. I never felt like an only child, although I was. I grew up in an atmosphere that taught you to be kind to other people and, maybe, even to go too far in helping the downtrodden. I suspect that some of the 'downtrodden' my family helped were just freeloaders.

"Growing up in that atmosphere, I guess, was why I was willing to put up with so much from Maceo."

3.

"I got pregnant and married when I was 16," Naomi said. "I had to finish school at Anacostia Evening High School. I didn't have much chance to go to college, because by the time I was 20 I had two daughters and a son. I stayed home with the children in the early years, but by the time I was 30, I had worked seven years with the Navy Department."

Like her mother, Naomi had married an alcoholic. Her husband, too, squandered the family's money. "He would show up at my workplace to get money from me, and I had to give it to him for fear of getting fired, because if he didn't get the money he would make a scene," she said. "Twice I tried to go to college in the evenings, but he kept showing up in my classrooms, too, and I had to drop out."

Naomi's husband had a penchant for grandiose gestures when he was drinking — gestures like showing up unannounced at his daughters' school and taking their entire classes to lunch at McDonald's. Incidents such as that embarrassed the daughters and tried Naomi's patience. At Parent-Teacher Organization meetings at the school, he would sit in a back row and start long rhetorical arguments with the speakers. "It got so I dreaded picking up my son and my daughters at school," Naomi recalled, "because every so often, someone would say to me, 'Guess what Mr. Daggs did today!' My daughter Nina's fourth-grade teacher — this would have been about 1967 — finally said to me, 'I wouldn't dream of telling you what to do, but you know it's not fair to let one person ruin five people's lives. If you need a safe harbor, you've got one with me.' I never forgot that, even though it took me five more years to get up the courage to act on her advice. I've given that same advice, along with the 'safe harbor' assurance, to some of my own students. I tell them, too, that my ex-husband benefited as well. He went to Alcoholic Anonymous and became a model grandfather."

When Naomi finally left her husband in 1972, she said, "I realized that I had to put some distance between us. I had relatives in California, and I had relatives in Richmond County. I picked Richmond County because it was close enough that the children could see their grandparents from time to time. Besides, one of Gloria Fisher's in-laws in Hamlet had just died, leaving a furnished house complete with linens and china, and Gloria said I could live there cheaply."

Naomi liquidated her retirement fund at the Navy Department and, with some financial assistance from her parents, she enrolled in Richmond Technical Institute (later Richmond Community College). She worked part-time in the school's public relations office, writing news releases for newspapers and radio, helping to design the school's catalog, and assisting with the prepation of promotional brochures and pamphlets. With the help of an English teacher at nearby Pembroke State College (later the University of North Carolina at Pembroke), she got a partial scholarship to attend the school,where she earned a degree in English. She came back to Richmond County to teach at Richmond Community College.

Those were hard years. "I never had a car until I finished college," she said. "I car-pooled to school, to work, everywhere. My children and I [the youngest child graduated from high school in 1978] had to learn what we could do without. Several times, I even played the stereotypical role of the Welfare Mom: Maceo would take me to buy groceries, I'd pay with food stamps, and we'd drive off in Maceo's Cadillac.

"But I was never beaten. The kids and I got help, but we would have made it somehow without help."

Naomi had seen a lot of Maceo since that first meeting on the sidewalk in Hamlet. The Fishers entertained often, and Maceo always seemed to wangle an invitation to their dinners and parties. Naomi began to see him elsewhere at parties, and in late 1972 they began to go out together. From 1973, she and Maceo were well nigh inseparable.

4.

But Maceo, still fond of playing the field when it came to women, did not want to marry and settle down until he had realized his dreams of an independent business and fortune. Naomi did not complain overmuch, because she knew how difficult domestic life would be for him — especially when, even years after her children grew up and moved away, Naomi was saddled with caring for her mother.

Naomi was not as sanguine about another factor influencing Maceo to delay marriage — his mother. To her mind, Vela was the decisive influence.

"Vela never approved of me," Naomi said. "After a while, she came to accept me to an extent, but she was still waiting for Maceo to find somebody more appropriate. She was chagrined that her son, with this grand future in front of him, had gotten involved with this wicked city woman — that's how she saw me — and a wicked city woman with three children, at that."

Naomi felt that Maceo was "a chameleon," always changing to adapt to his surroundings.

"Maceo felt comfortable anywhere," she said. "That's why people of all descriptions liked him. His ability to get along with people came from growing up in a business, where it was emphasized that you had to please everyone. That's one of the reasons he became such a flirt — he discovered that most women liked that.

"But Maceo was unconventional, too. His business didn't depend on white customers at all, but more of his close friends were white than black. He had a drive to fit in — everywhere. The reason he wanted so badly to fit in was that he really felt different from everybody else."

Attitudes about race and discrimination were one thing that set him apart, Naomi believed. Racist humor didn't seem to bother him, but underneath the surface, it made him seethe with anger. "I once asked him why, after somebody told a really racist joke at a party, he kept talking to the person, instead of walking away or protesting," Naomi said. "He told me, 'I don't have to protest. His telling the story told me what kind of person he was, and I know what kind of person I am.' He didn't go tilting at racist institutions, but tried to deal with people as individuals. Maceo just shut the man who told that racist joke out, from that point on."

Maceo was equally sensitive to what he regarded as racist behavior on the part of blacks. There was a flip side to his attitudes about racist humor, and that was that he loved to tell funny stories himself. Some of his stories poked gentle fun at black people, and he told these stories to whites. "He was breaking several codes by doing that," Naomi said. "One code said that that you didn't air the community's dirty laundry to white people. Another was that you didn't say anything to a white person that might be construed as derogatory toward blacks."

But to close friends who were white, like Prentice Taylor or Jimmy and Charles Maske, Maceo was capable of saying things like, "Another black man died last night — more money for me." Or he would regale the Maskes with the story of what his mother said to him after a funeral home employee, driving a

Maceo and Naomi Daggs
Photo from the collection of Naomi Daggs

hearse to Durham to pick up the body of someone who had died at Duke University Medical Center, collided with a car in Pittsboro, North Carolina, killing the driver of the car: "She called me and said, 'We're ruined. We're going to be wiped out financially. That dumb driver has killed a white man.' "

Naomi once went with Maceo to a pre-Homecoming Game party with some of his old college football teammates at North Carolina Central. "They had a lot of little rituals," she recalled. "Every homecoming, they'd meet at the home of a friend, and the friend's wife would cook up a mess of soul food. They'd all drink and tell stories, mostly about football. They had one ritual that involved singing Roger Miller's entire 'Chug-a-Lug' song, stopping every time they sang 'chug-a-lug' to toast somebody and have a drink. I felt uncomfortable, and I never went with him to another Homecoming party.

"But at some point, he realized that he had grown up, and these old football teammates were still kids at heart. He came back from one party and told me, 'It's kind of sad. They're still bemoaning the same racial injustices, the same kinds of discrimination that we talked about in college. It's time we moved beyond all that.'

"They had been talking a lot of separatist talk, and he didn't like that. He believed in an integrated society. He realized that they hadn't had the experience of having white friends, as he had — he gravitated toward white people, as part of that intense desire he had to fit in.

"Maceo felt like marches and protests were what we needed in the '60s, but they were not what we needed in the '70s and '80s. He wanted to see black people put themselves in places of power. He saw how other ethnic groups, like the Koreans, helped each other to reach those places of power, and he hoped that blacks would do the same. He really believed in the American Dream, and he thought economic status was the way to realize it. He wanted to be perceived as a person of strength, and he didn't like for blacks to make the case that we're victims."

5.

Maceo continued to see other women, throughout the nearly two decades of his relationship with Naomi.

"Every couple of years," she said, "he'd have a serious affair, and we'd break up. He'd always come back and throw himself on my mercy, apologizing and confessing that he was weak when it came to women but promising he'd never do it again. I'd believe him and think he was behaving himself for a while, until I saw some clues that he was having another affair. Eventually, when I found the clues, I'd just think to myself, 'He'll get through this one, too.' "

Maceo often didn't wait for Naomi to find out about the affairs; he told her about them.

"I filled a lot of roles for him," she said. "I was five years older, and I guess I was a kind of mother figure as well as a girlfriend. He felt he could trust his secrets with me. Whatever those secrets were, when things went sour for him, he knew we could still be friends."

When Naomi met Maceo, she said, "He was still in love with this girl he had known in Cincinnati. I guess it all started with that. I wasn't a serious relationship. I wasn't interfering with anything."

Eventually Naomi learned that there had been a third woman in Maceo's life in 1972. Since graduating from college, he had continued to date a woman occasionally, and in 1972 their relationship became more serious. The woman became pregnant and bore a daughter, telling Maceo that the baby was his. Maceo refused to marry the woman — he had no desire to settle into a domestic routine at his age — but he voluntarily paid her child support, keeping the arrangement a secret from his mother (but not from Naomi). He kept up the child support for several years, until, on the advice of his mother, he forced the issue of blood tests to determine paternity. The blood tests, performed at Duke University Medical Center in Durham, proved without doubt that the child was not his.

"The evening after he learned the results of the blood tests, we were at an Amway meeting," Naomi recalled, "and Maceo suddenly blurted out, 'You know that baby in Durham? That baby's not mine!' That's the way he was: Whatever was on his mind, he would say it."

(Later, the woman's father told Maceo that the child, now nearing her teen years, still believed that Maceo was her father. "That really troubled him," Naomi said. "He felt they hadn't been fair to her by not telling her the truth. He was determined to go talk to her himself, but I talked him out of it.")

Although that child was not his, Naomi believes that he may have had a child by a woman in Richmond County. "He felt me out, more than once, about his taking a child and my helping him raise it," she said.

6.

It wasn't the first time Maceo had suggested such a thing. He loved children.

Naomi's granddaughter Maleka, in 2001 a graduate student at New York University, is the daughter of Naomi's daughter Nina, who in the late 1980s was living in Fayetteville, North Carolina. "Maleka was always very precocious," Naomi said. "I called her my 'star child.' She and Maceo had a transcendent relationship. He just bonded with her. He used to have these long fatherly talks with her. He started calling me 'Ma-Ma,' because that's what Maleka called me. Maceo said to me, 'Why don't we just take Maleka? We could raise her.' I told him I couldn't take Maleka away from Nina, and besides, I wasn't about to start over again as a mother after having raised three children."

Maceo at Disney World
Photo from the collection of Naomi Daggs

One summer, Naomi and Maceo took Maleka to Disney World in Florida. "It was the happiest I ever saw Maceo," Naomi said. "He had had a fairly limited childhood, because his parents never took vacations, and he never got into things like comic books. 'I can't understand why they're supposed to be funny,' he told me. 'It's just made-up stuff.'

"But at Disney World, he was a child again, and he enjoyed doing everything that Maleka did. Nobody else was as much fun for him to be with. He went on all the rides with me, even though the Space Mountain ride scared him so much that he cried out, 'Oh, shit!' at one point. He kept apologizing to Maleka for that, but he told me, 'There ought to be a law against rides like that. It's dangerous. It could cause people to have heart attacks.'

"He taught Maleka to swim that week, in the motel swimming pool. When it came time for us to go, he asked me, 'Ma-Ma, can't we stay and watch the Electric Light Parade one more time?' We stayed."

Vela liked Maleka, too, but could never remember her name, calling her "Maketa." The next summer, Vela went with Maceo, Naomi and Maleka to tour Biltmore House, the Vanderbilt mansion in Asheville, North Carolina. The summer after that, they went to the North Carolina mountains for a week — minus Vela, who had not been impressed by Biltmore House.

"The Christmas before Maceo died," Naomi recalled, "Maleka wanted a Duke starter jacket for Christmas, and I was having trouble finding one that I could afford on my budget. Maceo told me, 'Whatever it costs, if Maleka wants it, you get it. I'll help pay for it.'

"Maleka still misses him."

7.

Maceo's most serious love affair started at one of those Homecoming reunions in Durham. There, Maceo met a woman he had dated in the late 1970s, and they began dating again.

"That woman thought Maceo had more money than he did — that same little trap again," Naomi said scornfully. "But Vela was pushing Maceo to get engaged to her, and finally he did. He told me about her. But we still continued to see each other. We'd eat together, watch TV, wash the dogs, work with Maceo's horses. It was just that, to my mind at least, ours wasn't a romantic relationship any longer. With Maceo engaged, we were just friends."

Naomi took a trip to New York City and ran into a man she had once dated. They went out to dinner together. When Naomi returned home, she told Maceo about the chance encounter and the dinner date.

"I didn't think it would bother him — he was engaged to somebody else, after all — but he just went berserk," she said. "I had never seen him like that."

It was the beginning of what Naomi called "the scariest period of my life."

"He held me like a hostage in my house," she said. "He was threatening me. I finally had to leave town; I took a leave of absence for a couple of months, to let Maceo cool down. I stayed with a friend of a friend in Charlotte.

"Once, during the time I was staying in Charlotte, I went to Fayetteville to visit my daughters. My son-in-law told me that Maceo had just left. 'I don't know when he ate, or when he went to the bathroom,' he told me. 'He's been out there in his car for a week, waiting for you to show up.'

"Gloria [Fisher] called me several times in Charlotte to tell me that Maceo had been calling her every day, demanding to know where I was. She finally got me to talk to him on the phone. He talked me into coming back. But things weren't any better when I got back."

Naomi's health complicated matters. After an emergency hysterectomy, she went to Washington to recover and stayed there, with her father and grandfather, during a lengthy recuperation fraught with complications. When she came back to Richmond County, she moved in temporarily with another "friend of a friend," a woman from Sanford, North Carolina, who had recently moved to Hamlet. The woman's husband was still in Sanford, wrapping up some unfinished business before joining her.

One weekend the woman paid a visit to her husband in Sanford, and Naomi went along. They found Maceo at the husband's house, waiting for them.

Maceo talked Naomi into coming back to Hamlet with him. "Halfway to Hamlet," she said, "he pulled off the road and pulled a gun on me. I was scared to death. I don't remember what he asked, and I don't remember anything I said in response. But he finally told me, 'You've said all the right things,' and he put the gun away and we drove back to Hamlet.

"He broke off his engagement to the woman in Durham, and after that, things returned to normal with us. He told me, 'I just thought I could go on and get married and I'd still have you, just like it always was. You know I'm weak, Ma-Ma.'"

"But the last woman I stayed with —the one from Sanford — Maceo never confessed to it, but I'm sure it was he that put soap in that woman's gas tank a week or so after I returned to Hamlet and ruined her car. It would have been Amway soap, of course."

8.

"It's hard to believe that Maceo's been gone for ten years," Naomi said. "Everybody who knew him feels the same way.

"The hurt gets better as time goes on. But for the first five or six years, it seemed to me that it had only been a few days since Maceo was killed.

"You can't stay sad, though, if you think about him for long, because you always think of something amusing about him."

VII.

APRIL 12-13, 1991

1.

Most of what is known about the activities of Bobbie and Joey Caldwell on April 12, 1991, comes from Bobbie's court testimony and her statements to investigators. Her version of events is suspect, since she was a participant in the crimes — but, once she started telling the truth to investigators, they were never able to catch her in a lie or a contradiction. Her version of events is probably accurate.

The Caldwells slept late, as they often did, on the morning of April 12.

About 9:15 a.m., shortly after Maceo arrived for work at the McEachern Funeral Home in Rockingham, Bobbie telephoned him, asking if he would be around later to look at a van that he might be interested in buying. The van, she said, could have "Pro-Formance" painted on its sides and would thus serve as an advertisement as well as a means to haul cases of the sports drink to retail locations. Maceo told her that he would be around until the evening hours, because he had to prepare a body for burial the next day.

Joey unscrewed the light bulb in his garage door, so that it would not come on automatically that night when he drove into the driveway; neighbors could be watching.

The Caldwells drove to Charlotte in separate cars — he in the Acura, which was registered to her; she in the BMW, which was registered in his name — and spent some time at a tanning parlor that they frequently used. They ate hamburgers at a fast-food restaurant. They then drove to a YMCA on Morehead Street, where they frequently worked out. They signed in, using their electronic identification cards so that their presence would be on record. Moments later, Joey and Bobbie walked out a side door — the Y did not require clients to sign out — and Bobbie walked him to the Acura. Joey got in and drove away, and Bobbie reentered the Y through the side door and worked out.

Joey drove to Hamlet, settling in beside Vela McEachern's driveway to wait. He would probably have arrived there, given normal traffic conditions, about 3:45 p.m., hoping to kill the McEacherns quickly and return to Charlotte by early evening. But no one reported seeing him there until later in the afternoon, near 5 p.m. Had he driven aimlessly around Richmond County, steeling himself for what he was about to do and waiting until it was time for Vela to arrive home?

There is another possibility. Joey would have had to stop somewhere on the way from Charlotte to Hamlet to change into the loose clothing and floppy boots he wore in Hamlet, and to change the license plate on the Acura. He might also have put a temporary color rinse on his dark hair, since some who reported seeing him described his hair as "sandy." He could have changed and colored his hair in a service station restroom, but that might have called attention to him. A more likely possibility is that he checked into a motel on the way under a false name, paid in cash, changed his clothes and dyed his hair, and left his key in the room for a maid to find the next morning.

Police, convinced that the killer had not lingered in the area after the shootings, did not think to check motel registrations or show photographs of their two suspects, Caldwell and Sullivan, to motel clerks.

However Joey spent the time from 3:45 p.m. until about 5 p.m., there is no question that, from the time of the 9:15 a.m. phone call, he knew that he would kill Vela as well as Maceo. Since Maceo planned to work at the funeral home until late in the evening, Joey would have to use Vela as "bait" to bring Maceo to the house. She would have to be killed too, so that there would be no witness to Maceo's' murder. It is unclear whether Bobbie realized this as well.

Bobbie left the YMCA at 3:30 p.m. and drove to Park Road Shopping Center in Charlotte. She bought two tickets to the 4:15 p.m. showing of the movie "Class Action" at Park Terrace Cinema, which Joey had seen with her earlier in the week and could talk about knowledgeably if anyone questioned his claim that he had seen it. After watching the movie, Bobbie drove to a nearby First Union National Bank parking lot where, if Joey had returned to Charlotte by that time, they had agreed to meet. She waited a while in the parking lot, but when she saw no sign of Joey, she drove across the street to the huge Southpark Mall shopping center.

At Southpark, Bobbie bought toothpaste at an Eckerd Drug store, making sure to get a receipt showing the time of sale — 7:17 p.m. She bought toiletries at a Casual Lassie store and a cup of coffee at a gourmet coffee shop called Gloria Jean's. She drank the coffee while sitting on a bench in the commons area of the mall. The Charlotte Symphony was giving a free concert in the commons area at the time, and she listened for a while.

At about the time Bobbie was driving to the First Union lot, Joey was holding a gun to Vela's head, forcing her to call Maceo and ask him to come home because she was sick. When the conversation ended, he yanked the telephone cord out of the wall in the McEacherns' kitchen.

Vela began "jabbering" (Joey's word) with fright. Joey picked up a frying pan from the kitchen range, pushed her through a doorway and a short hallway into the den, pushed her into a chair, and hit her over the head with the pan. The blow stunned her, and the frying pan shattered.

"People have asked me," said Terry Moore, "how he could have hit her hard enough to break a frying pan, and not kill her. It was a thin metal frying pan to begin with — not one of those cast-iron jobs — and repeated heating and cooling had made the metal brittle. No question, it was a terrific blow he hit her, but that frying pan was not as hard to break as you might think."

Joey later told Bobbie that he had only hit the kitchen wall with the frying pan, to frighten Vela enough to quieten her, and that only the handle had broken. Only weeks later did he tell her the true story.

When Maceo arrived at his mother's home, he saw Joey's car next to the driveway and started to back his car up, apparently intending to leave. Joey told Vela to go onto the front stoop with him and tell Maceo that it was "all right," that Joey only had some new Pro-Formance flavors that he wanted to show Maceo. She followed his orders.

Many Richmond Countians have wondered why Vela didn't warn Maceo at this time or earlier, on the phone, saying something like, "Joey Caldwell's here, and he's got a gun! Call the police!" That would have put Joey in an untenable situation, certainly — but given his emotional state at the time, he might still have killed Vela. In any case, Vela was understandably frightened and doubtless clung to a hope that Maceo, the strong son on whom she had long depended, could talk Joey out of any violent act he might be planning.

Joey ordered Maceo into the den and made him sit on the sofa. Vela sat in the easy chair about eight feet away from the sofa.

Then, incredibly, Joey sat on the fireplace hearth, holding the shotgun, and began apologizing for what he was about to do. Maceo sat nearby in the sofa, at right angles to the hearth. Vela's easy chair faced the hearth, but across the room, in a corner beyond the sofa.

Joey told Bobbie he began talking calmly but as he proceeded worked himself into a rage at the McEacherns — possibly "psyching himself up" for the murders.

Joey had to kill Maceo for the life insurance money, he said. He was in debt and needed the money to stay in business. There was no other way. Vela had to die because she had seen him and could convict him as a witness. He spoke for several minutes, detailing his various debts and repeatedly saying he was sorry.

Maceo reasoned desperately with Joey. He would lend him the money to pay off his immediate debts, he said. He would increase his regular payments for the Pro-Formance distribution rights.

"I'll do anything you want," he said.

Joey stood up and walked toward Maceo until he was about four feet away. He shot Maceo in the chest, then turned quickly and shot Vela in the torso and hip. "I was about as far from her as the width of a restaurant booth," Joey later told Bobbie.

"The first shots killed them instantly," said Terry Moore. "You could tell, because they didn't do much bleeding. There was not nearly as much blood as you sometimes see in these cases."

(Later, Joey became indignant when an SBI agent told the Caldwells about the "messy scene" in Vela's house after the murders. "It wasn't messy at all," Bobbie said Joey told her.)

It would have been obvious to all but the most casual observer that both McEacherns were dead — killed by the shots to their chests. But Joey had to make sure. He removed the spent shell casings from the shotgun, put them in his pocket, and reloaded. Stepping closer to his victims, he fired shots into Maceo's and Vela's faces.

He walked back to his car, again carrying his weapons in a box. He placed the box in the car and drove back to Belmont, a trip of more than 100 miles, being careful to observe all traffic laws. (But he still had the Ontario plate on the car, unusual enough that it could have gotten him pulled over by a curious law enforcement officer.) He changed clothes in his car and threw his camo clothes and his oversize boots — chosen in order to leave misleading footprints for investigators —over bridges and into the water at several locations. Possibly he discarded some of the clothing as he drove over the Pee Dee River separating Richmond from Anson counties, possibly as he drove over the Catawba River separating Mecklenburg and Gaston counties. He also threw into the water the guns, the box and the Canadian license plate.

A later reference that Joey made to the evidence being "scattered," and Bobbie's response — "Yeah, in the lakes and everywhere" — indicates that Joey may have driven past several inlets and coves on Lake Norman near the Caldwells' home, throwing the clothing, weapon, and other evidence into the lake.

None of this evidence was ever recovered.

Joey was already on the road back home when Bobbie left Southpark Mall about 8:30 p.m. She drove home to Belmont. She put the Eckerd receipt and the movie ticket stubs into a belted wallet — a "fanny pack" — that Joey often wore. She telephoned her mother in Belmont; her sister in Blacksburg, Virginia; and a friend in nearby Huntersville. The friend was not at home; Bobbie left a message on her answering machine. In her conversations with her mother and sister, she said things to indicate that Joey was in the house — even asking him questions. (She had done the same thing on April 10.) Then she taped episodes of *Dallas* and *True Detectives* and part of the *Arsenio Hall Show*. Joey could watch the tapes and tell investigators convincingly that he had seen the shows in real time.

Returning home about 11:15, Joey drove into his garage. Bobbie met him at the door. He looked downward and nodded his head in a "Yes" gesture.

"Was he alone?" she asked.

"No," Joey said.

2.

Joey gave his clothing — the clothing he had changed into in the car — to Bobbie to launder, to remove any possible trace evidence. He took a shower, for the same purpose — and perhaps to wash the "sandy" dye out of his dark hair. He watched the TV programs Bobbie had taped. At about 2 a.m., the Caldwells went to bed.

They were still awake when the phone rang at 2:30. They didn't answer, but let the answering machine take the call. They left their bedroom and went downstairs to the kitchen, where the answering machine sat, to play back the tape.

The call had been from Drew Carver, to tell them that Maceo was dead.

3.

Joey told Bobbie that he wished the original plan had remained in place and that he had been able to get the insurance proceeds by killing Clyde Sullivan.

Bobbie claimed that, before he left for Hamlet on April 12, he told her, "I'm sorry it has to be Maceo. I like Maceo."

4.

The Caldwells were up early on the morning of April 13, despite their late bedtime. They had much to do.

Joey called his Gymbags attorney, informing him of Maceo's death and asking him to take the documents relating to the Sullivan lawsuit to the Hamlet Police Department.

He went into the garage and put the North Carolina license plate and two Pro-Formance bumper stickers on the Acura. He hoped that anyone who might have taken note of the car beside Vela McEachern's driveway would have noticed that it had not had bumper stickers. He removed the metallic tape stripes from the car, along with the brown tape that had covered the Acura emblems, and burned the tape.

Some time before, Joey had bought some long-distance electronic listening devices, and he thought that they might throw him under suspicion if law officers came to the house to interview him and noticed them. He gathered the devices together and put them into the Acura. The Caldwells left together in the Acura, and Joey drove to a vacant lot next to the Harris Teeter grocery store in Belmont and threw the devices into a kudzu-choked ravine.

Across the street from the Harris Teeter was a Wendy's hamburger restaurant. The Caldwells ate lunch there and returned home. On the way, Joey stopped the car near South Point High School in Belmont, took a cup of water that he had asked for before leaving Wendy's, and threw the water on the Acura's bumper stickers; his idea was that road grime would stick to the damp bumper stickers, making them look as if they had been placed on the car earlier than that morning.

Upon returning home, he replaced the light in the garage door. He asked Bobbie to wipe down the interior of the car with rubbing alcohol and to do the same with the Acura emblems on the car's exterior, to remove any sticky tape residue.

The work had barely been completed when SBI Special Agents Leroy Allen and Bill Lane and another agent, identified later by Bobbie as "Agent Reichert," showed up. Joey showed them the movie ticket stubs and the Eckerd receipt. He told them about working out at the Y, about the telephone calls Bobbie had made, about *True Detectives* and *Dallas* and *Arsenio*. He invited them to search the premises for guns or other evidence.

The agents left, after fingerprinting the Caldwells, taking photographs of them, checking out the Acura thoroughly, and subjecting the Caldwells to a grueling four hours of questions — but they were not satisfied. They realized that Joey's alibi would fall apart if they could prove that Bobbie had been his confederate. They began considering whether Bobbie Caldwell had set up the alibi for her husband.

They were to return many more times in the next year, interviewing both Caldwells at length.

One of them, they reasoned, was bound to break — sooner or later.

VIII.

INVESTIGATION

1.

The McEachern murders challenged the resources of the tiny Hamlet Police Department, requiring its officers to chase down leads in far-flung corners of the state.

"There's a good word for how this case affected the department," Chief Terry Moore said. "The word is 'overburdened.' The case went in all different directions. It's not like, 'Who's going to interview the ones on Bauersfeld Street, and who's going to interview the ones that live down Highway 177?' It's, 'What side of the state do you want?'

"The SBI committed itself to the case early on. The agents suggested that we put all the leads we obtained on a computer and then decide who would go where, who would handle the evidence, etc.

"Some things, we knew we had to do right away. I put some calls in to Canada and had them check border crossings for vehicles fitting the description of that dark green Honda or Acura. We put out all-point bulletins on the vehicle. We got one call back, saying that a Highway Patrol trooper had seen a car like that around Matthews that night."

Matthews, in Union County, is somewhat more than halfway between the McEachern home and the Caldwells' home near the Gaston County town of Belmont. That pointed to Caldwell as possibly being the murderer, but the sighting by itself didn't prove anything. There were a lot of dark green Hondas and Acuras. The state trooper didn't recall whether the car he had seen had had an Ontario license plate — he knew only that it wasn't a North Carolina plate.

"The SBI," Moore said, "checked with the North Carolina Department of Motor Vehicles, to see if any kind of tag like that (Canadian license plate) had ever been stolen in the area. (Hamlet police officer) Gerald Sellers and I spent a lot of time calling car dealers about sales of dark green Hondas and Acuras.

"And, boy, did we ever want to get a tag number of that Ontario plate! We even had a specialist in hypnotism with the North Carolina Justice Academy, hypnotize two people who had seen the car up close, hoping that they would be able under hypnotism to remember even part of the number.

"Nothing panned out."

2.

During the first week after the murders, the Hamlet police interviewed dozens of people. Naomi Daggs was one of the first.

"Naomi was all torn up about Maceo's death, naturally," Moore said. "But in our first interview with her, she was very unemotional and matter-of-fact and mature about the whole thing. She was secure in the knowledge that she had been Maceo's true love — but she knew Maceo wasn't perfect. She knew he had always had an eye for the ladies, and she knew that he had dated other women.

"There had been a lot of women in Maceo's life, and Naomi knew who many of them were — and told us. A man with Maceo's history, we couldn't discount the possibility that his murder had been a crime of passion. We had to check out these other women and their husbands and boyfriends."

Moore especially remembered one trip that he and Hamlet police officers Jim Thomas and Gerald Sellers and Assistant Chief Robert Bristow had taken to South Carolina, "four or five days" after the murders.

"We had already been on several wild goose chases of this sort and other sorts — we were told that Maceo was killed over a drug deal, all sorts of things — but we had to follow up every lead," Moore explained. "We had heard that some lady in Hamlet had had problems with her husband over dating Maceo. We found the woman and her husband living in South Carolina, and we drove down there."

Moore felt a chill go down his spine when the pair drove up in front of the couple's home. Parked in front of the house was a dark green late-model Honda. "What our heart rates would have been like when we went down there and saw that car, I can't begin to tell you," he said.

"The woman was very cooperative," Moore went on. "She was good-natured and mature, and she volunteered to let us take pictures of the car. She convinced us totally that it had all been a malicious rumor with no foundation in fact.

"She didn't know Maceo from Adam's house cat."

3.

The police also interviewed other women Maceo had dated, as well as friends of the McEacherns, relatives, employees and former employees, business associates and acquaintances in Southern Pines and Fayetteville and Fort Bragg, where

Maceo had distributed Amway products and Pro-Formance. "A lot of this stuff winds up meaning nothing," Moore said, "but the bottom line is, you have to do it or you might miss something important."

The police — Moore, especially — granted dozens of interviews to reporters from the Richmond County Daily Journal, which blanketed Richmond County with its circulation; The Charlotte Observer, which circulated statewide; and other newspapers.

"We worked in concert with the press," Moore said. "The reporters were helpful to us by keeping those articles going in the paper. It was part of our proactive strategy, to let the killer know that we were still on the hunt, keeping the pressure on so that, we hoped, he would break down. The Charlotte Observer was particularly helpful in that regard, because its stories ran on the business pages; that in itself was indicative that the police thought the killings were business-related.

"But there were things we held back from the press, as we always do in a murder investigation — things that only we and the murderer could know about: the broken frying pan, the concrete block, the wadding from the shotgun cells, the phone cord being torn out of the wall. If someone ever came forward and had that information, we'd know that he or she had talked with the murderer."

4.

In the course of his training at FBI headquarters in Quantico, Moore had become good friends with Robert K. Ressler, the FBI special agent (now retired) who founded the FBI's Behavioral Science Unit and was instrumental, with "Mindhunter" John Douglas and others, in developing the infant science of criminal profiling. FBI specialists in profiling studied evidence gathered in crime investigations and developed psychological and demographic "profiles" of the likely perpetrators. If the profiles were on the money, which they were in an astounding number of cases, they could help local police departments narrow down their rosters of suspects — by eliminating suspects who didn't fit the profile.

But there was a danger in dependence on profiling. If the profiles were inaccurate, which they had been in a number of highly publicized cases — notably the Atlanta child murders of the 1980s, when FBI profilers predicted that the murderer, when apprehended, would be a white man — they might throw investigators off the track and keep them from giving sufficient attention to viable suspects who didn't fit the profiles.

Moore, whose investigation had already reached a number of dead ends within a few days after the McEachern murders, was willing to take that chance. He called Ressler and other friends at the Bureau and obtained from them an agreement to profile the killer.

It was a rare concession on the part of the overworked Behavioral Science Unit, whose members preferred to spend their time profiling serial criminals who tend to follow a pattern in carrying out repetitive crimes of violence. Their preference stemmed from two factors. First, apprehending serial criminals was important in that it would prevent their committing additional crimes. Second, as Moore said, "Lust/sex pattern-type cases give them more material for profiling, and they can generally come up with better, fuller profiles in that type of case than in the type of case we had, which looked like murder for profit. Still, almost all cases can be profiled, and you can usually get something from the profile that you can use."

Moore obtained an FBI Violent Criminals Apprehension Program (VICAP) form from SBI Special Agent Doug Greene in Rockingham. He filled out the form in exhaustive detail, listing everything that the Hamlet police and the SBI had learned to date about the McEachern killings, and he faxed a copy of the filled-out VICAP form to Quantico. A few days later, an FBI special agent arrived in Hamlet to study the physical evidence, interview investigators, and draw up a profile.

He couldn't do it. The killer had not left enough evidence behind for the profiler to get a handle on his personality. Based purely on the circumstantial evidence in the murders, the killer could be anyone.

"Sorry," the FBI man told Moore. "You got yourself a tough case here."

As if Moore didn't know that already.

5.

But the tough little chief was not discouraged. "To me," he said, "investigating crimes is almost a religious type of thing. I've always felt that, if you work hard enough on it, you will be rewarded.

"Here's a good example of what I'm talking about. A few years ago, we investigated a break-in in Hamlet. We investigated that thing for months, and we turned up nothing. But we kept working on it, as hard as we could. Finally, we found one silver dollar that we could prove had been taken in the break-in. And that silver dollar led us to suspects in Georgia, Florida, and California. We finally arrested the whole gang. I think the hand of God was with us on that case."

Moore vowed to keep working hard on the McEachern murders, putting every ounce of his department's resources, every available man-hour, into the grinding task.

Many of the leads the department pursued were dead ends almost from the beginning.

"We concentrated from the start on Sullivan and Caldwell," Moore said.

"But we couldn't find a good lead that would pin the crime on either of them, and in the meantime we were getting all kinds of goofy tips that we had to check out — because, you never know, some goofy tip might just have a germ of truth in it.

"It hurt that, because we went so long without making an arrest, the public felt that we had stopped trying. Eight months into the case, people would say to me, 'You guys just gave up on the McEachern case, didn't you?' But we couldn't worry about the public perception. If we let everybody know everything we were doing, in order to save our reputations because we were worried about what people thought — well, we wouldn't have been doing what was right for the victims."

But police can't work on even the highest-profile cases in a vacuum. By the end of 1991, the Hamlet police had investigated another double murder case and a fatal nightclub stabbing, as well as a disastrous fire. The year 1991 turned out to be the worst year, in terms of violent deaths, in Richmond County since 1886, when a tornado had ripped through the rural community of Philadelphia north of Rockingham and killed more than 60 people.

Fifty-four persons were murdered or killed in accidents in Richmond County in 1991. Twenty-five of them died and fifty-four others suffered injuries — many disabling and permanent — on September 3, when natural gas from a ruptured gas line in the Imperial Food Products, Inc., plant in Hamlet, a poultry-processing plant, caught a spark from a welder's torch. The fire spread quickly to vats of hot grease in which chicken parts were cooking. Many panicked employees rushed to a fire door in the rear of the plant only to discover that it was locked — an illegal action that, court records later showed, was ordered by the plant's owner, elderly Mississippian Emmett Roe, to forestall suspected employee thefts. When firefighters fought through the flames and finally reached the back door, they found fourteen of the employees' bodies piled in a heap. The metal door showed foot-shaped dents, evidence that someone had desperately tried to kick the door open. Even that would have done no good; someone had parked an Imperial Food Products truck so near the door that it could not have been opened sufficiently to allow anyone to squeeze through. In all, twenty-four employees and a route man for a snack company, who had been filling coin-operated machines in the plant's canteen, died of smoke inhalation. Roe was later convicted of manslaughter and sent to prison. The tragedy resulted in sweeping legislation on workplace safety in North Carolina and stepped-up safety inspections by state officials.

"The state took control of the Imperial Food fire investigation," Moore said, "and we didn't have much to do with it except for helping to coordinate the activities of various state agencies and dealing with victims' relief organizations. Still, it all took time. And by that time, we also had another double homicide and any number of other crimes to investigate."

On the morning of August 23, clerks arrived for work at The Pantry, a convenience store on Highway 177 south in Hamlet, and found the door unlocked and the cash missing from the register. Quick checks by the police showed that the night clerk, 21-year-old Amos Weatherford, and his roommate, 26-year-old Paul Callahan, were missing. Police theorized that the pair had stolen the money from the register and skipped town.

But three days later, the police learned that a Cambridge, Maryland, man, John Lee Conaway, 24, had been arrested in Cambridge for firing a handgun on a public street. The car Conaway had been driving was registered to Paul Callahan. Based on evidence found in the car, police in Hamlet charged Conaway with the armed robberies of three stores in Hamlet.

Then, three days after that, the bodies of Weatherford and Callahan were found in a wooded area off Old Laurinburg Road near Hamlet. Both had been shot. Weatherford had been married and had a young child, born with a congenital heart condition, who needed extensive medical care; the child's mother could no longer rely on child support to help meet the steep medical bills.

Police charged Conaway with two counts of murder, two counts of kidnapping, and the larceny of Callahan's car. Three 19-year-olds — two from Hamlet, one from Durham, North Carolina — who had allegedly accompanied Conaway in Callahan's car to Maryland were charged with being accessories after the fact to Conaway's crimes.

All four suspects were in custody within little more than a week after the murders, but police still had the job of interviewing the suspects, gathering additional evidence, and testifying at the trials of the four men — not to mention doing their best to placate the families of the murdered men, who felt that the police had not pushed their investigation hard enough in the early going.

"It all stretched us pretty thin," Moore said.

"In the meantime, though, we wanted the McEacherns' family and close friends to know that we were still on the case. We got them in (to the police station), told them what the problems were, what we could and couldn't do, and what they could reasonably expect. We let them know that leads were thin — we even showed some of them our 'lead sheets' — but that we were determined never to give up. In police work you find, if you don't do that sort of thing, the families of the victims quickly become alienated from you, which makes the cases even more difficult to work."

6.

The SBI pitched in by assigning two agents full-time to the case — and Henry Poole, head of the Bureau's elite Murders Unsolved Team (MUST), delayed his retirement in hope that he could help bring the killers of the McEacherns to justice.

"At various times, the SBI sent at least twelve different agents down here," Moore said. "It might have been as many as fourteen or fifteen. (SBI Director) Charles Dunn even came down himself, to tell me he had assigned Bill Lane and Leroy Allen full-time to the case. They were ideal choices. Bill lived up there (Gaston County, where the Caldwells lived), and Leroy wasn't married and didn't have any objection to spending long hours away from home. And both men were top-flight investigators. That was really the big break in the case."

Still, as the months wore on, any hope of bringing the killer to justice seemed ever more quixotic. The investigation ultimately took the lawmen to four states, but they kept running into dead ends.

The U.S. Attorney's Office in Greensboro entered the investigation. Officials in that agency agreed to help investigate the case because the murderer had driven a car with a Canadian license plate. That could mean that he had crossed state lines to commit a felony — a federal offense.

Assistant U.S. Attorney Rick Glaser was a slight, balding man with tons of nervous energy. He and his SBI liaison, Special Agent Bill Lane, made a curious Mutt-and-Jeff team: Lane was portly and disheveled. Lane told Glaser that he and Allen had never been able to interview Bobbie out of the presence of her husband.

Glaser knew how that could be accomplished: a federal grand jury.

Unlike state grand juries, which exist primarily to indict suspects, a federal grand jury has broad investigative powers. And it can question witnesses in secret, with no defense attorneys allowed to be present. That meant that Joey would not know what his wife was telling the grand jury.

There was another huge advantage to the federal courts' intervention in the case. It was beginning to look as though the investigators would never come up with enough evidence to charge Caldwell with murder in the state courts, because his wife could not testify against him in the state courts. But there is no "spousal privilege" in the federal courts: There, a spouse can legally testify against a spouse. In federal court, Caldwell could be charged with federal weapons offenses and — more important, from the standpoint of Glaser and the other investigators — with money laundering, and if convicted, he could possibly be put away for life.

"Money laundering" can be defined as any use of funds that have been illegally obtained. If Glaser could prove, to a jury's satisfaction, that Caldwell had murdered the McEacherns, he would simultaneously prove that Caldwell had obtained the insurance money through an illegal act. And Caldwell could be charged with money laundering each time he spent any part of the funds — or even if he transferred part of the funds from one bank to another.

Federal prison sentences are served "day for day," with no possibility of parole. If Caldwell were to be sentenced, say, to one year on each of 50 counts of money laundering, he would never again see the outside of a prison.

7.

James M. Cain's 1936 novella "Double Indemnity" tells the story of a man and a woman who murder the woman's husband for his life insurance. In the end, the pair commit suicide.

Some critics dismissed the book as a sensationalistic potboiler, but Cain said it embodied a moral lesson: "That two people can not do what these people did, and stand to live with each other."

Joey and Bobbie Caldwell learned that lesson the hard way.

Joey had left few clues at the murder scene, and Bobbie had taken pains to establish an alibi for Joey — but investigators for the Hamlet Police Department and the State Bureau of Investigation came to believe that the alibi was a ruse. They began to look harder at the Caldwells as suspects in the murders, suspecting that Bobbie had conspired with her husband.

They grew more suspicious of her after a Charlotte attorney approached the U.S. Attorney's office in Greensboro, seeking to trade testimony in the case in return for immunity from prosecution for his client, whom he called "Client X."

The grand jury called Bobbie Caldwell twice to testify — once in October 1992, and again in February of 1993. Between the two appearances, Joey had broached the subject of a large insurance policy on Bobbie's life, and Bobbie had become suspicious of her husband's motives and fearful of what might happen to her if she could not break free of him.

Breaking free of Joey was a tall order. Joey was obsessed with his wife and rarely let her out of his sight except when she was at her teaching job. But on the pretext of running an errand, she dashed into the attorney's office one day and laid out her proposal. She had decided to testify against her husband, she said, because she feared his temper — and because, with the $2 million already almost gone, just seventeen months after the murders, Joey had lately asked her to take out a large life insurance policy.

Client X, the investigators figured, had to be either Bobbie Caldwell or Barbara Sullivan, wife of Clyde Sullivan. But the communication from "Clint X's" attorney — called a "proffer" in legal terminology — said that Client X had lied about the murderer's whereabouts on the day of the crime. Barbara Sullivan had not told investigators anything about Clyde Sullivan's whereabouts on April 12, 1991.

The proffer also said that Client X could testify that the murderer took a lie-detector test under the influence of drugs, which were designed to throw off the polygraph readings. The investigators knew that Sullivan had refused a lie-detector test but that Joey Caldwell had taken a private polygraph exam at his own expense.

Client X had to be Bobbie Caldwell.

And that meant that Joey Caldwell had to be the murderer.

8.

Less than two years after the murders, the Caldwells had already spent the $2 million.

Much of it went to pay debts. A total of $1,358,080 went to pay back dividends owed to stockholders in Gymbags — but $1,020,000 of those dividends went to Bobbie. Clyde Sullivan and his wife Barbara Sullivan collected $50,400 each, and their son Lee Sullivan collected $75,040. Oddly, Steve Smith, Gymbags' accountant, collected only $49,500, although his percentage interest in the company was the same as the Sullivans'. Randy Riggins got $9,990 for his 1.1 percent share of the stock, as did distributor Ben Rudisill. Three other stockholders — Vince Harrelson, Jeff Bridges, and Lewis Bridges — collected a total of $49,950.

Calling the payments to the Sullivans — except for one $25,000 dividend to Lee Sullivan — "dividends" was not strictly correct, however. The $151,200 paid to the three Sullivans compensated them in total for their original stock purchases, in settlement of Clyde Sullivan's countersuit against the Caldwells over the Pro-Formance distribution rights. By killing Maceo, Joey had killed the Caldwells' key witness in the lawsuit hearing, and he and Bobbie were forced to settle the suit on terms largely dictated by Sullivan.

The Caldwells also, from the insurance proceeds, paid themselves a total of $52,623.35 in back salaries.

Another $199,564.08 went to pay the bills for radio advertising and for Gymbags' advertising agency.

A total of $34,024.30 was used to pay attorney fees the Caldwells had owed.

Vitamin Locker, Joey Caldwell's former business, still had debts. The Caldwells paid out $11,406.61 to settle a court judgment for an office lease on which Vitamin Locker had defaulted. They paid $42,350.78 to the Internal Revenue Service for Vitamin Locker's back taxes, interest, and penalties. They used another $34,210.88 to pay off a bank loan to Vitamin Locker. They paid $14,269.78 for a lease on a copier they had used at Vitamin Locker.

Still another $21,997.70 went to pay off a loan that Bobbie claimed had been taken out for her mother's benefit.

Then came the self-indulgent expenses, and there were plenty of those.

The Caldwells bought four vehicles: a Mercedes ($96,765.84), a Porsche ($78,985.50), a Jeep ($19,697), and a boat (approximately $27,000). They later traded the Jeep for a more expensive Ford Explorer, and they traded the Mercedes for a Cadillac. They bought $22,584.94 worth of furniture from two Charlotte stores. And they shelled out $150,000 for a 2,000-square-foot addition to their 3,000-square-foot house — more than the house had cost them originally. The addition contained an office, a weight room (which the Caldwells furnished with $17,741.20 worth of workout equipment), a room for a pool table, and a warehouse area where Joey housed the inventory for another nutritional-supplement business he was starting, called Nutrin Labs.

Add all that together, less the money the Caldwells paid themselves, and it comes out to $1,138,000. A big chunk of the $2 million was left — but to understand how the Caldwells could go through it in a year, one must understand the scale of their day-to-day expenses.

They had to pay property taxes on $300,000 worth of house and well over $200,000 worth of vehicles. They had to make payments on the original $140,000 house they had bought in 1990. They had to rent a boathouse at a nearby marina to house Joey's boat. They had to buy a pool table and ancillary equipment to furnish the room they had built for that purpose. The utility bills on their huge house would not have been insignificant. Nor would maintenance costs on the Caldwells' house, their vehicles, and their large, manicured lawn. The house and the lawn were dotted with expensive security devices.

A major chunk of the Caldwells' funds went to pay insurance premiums. They had homeowners' insurance, business liability insurance and a group hospitalization plan, liability and collision and comprehensive insurance on their vehicles, and a total of $7 million worth of expensive "whole life" insurance policies.

They ate almost every meal out, entertained lavishly at Christmas and gave expensive gifts to each other and to friends and business associates. They had the dogs groomed weekly, added to Bobbie's collection of collector plates, and bought clothing. Some mornings, when Joey stepped out of his house, he was wearing $3,000 worth of clothing and jewelry.

Then there were the startup costs for the new business: buying inventory, advertising and distribution costs, telemarketing costs. These would have been considerable, even though by this time Joey and Bobbie were the only employees (Joey doing business, even with a gym in Belmont, under the name "Albert Adams," so that Nutrin Labs would not be tainted by word of his previous business failures).

By early 1993, the money was gone — with the exception of $4,500 some SBI agents found in a green bag in a desk drawer in his home office, about

$25,000 worth of stocks and bonds (which investigators found a receipt for, but creditors have never located), and (one relative said) perhaps $160,000 or more that Bobbie had surreptitiously drawn out of the Caldwells' joint accounts and hidden away.

The Caldwells' only secure income was the small salary Bobbie made as a teacher in a Charlotte middle school — a job she had taken on Aug. 11, 1992, after it became apparent that she and Joey could not make it for long without some alternative source of income.

And Joey still owed back property taxes on some land he owned in Gaston County.

9.

Bobbie was concerned about the large amount of life insurance that Joey was asking her to take out.

They had let their two $3.5 million policies lapse in December 1992, because they could no longer afford to pay the premiums.

In one conversation with her ex-husband Randy Riggins about that time, according to Riggins' recollection, Bobbie said, "I don't know why we have two and a half million (*sic*) dollars' worth of insurance on each other. Wouldn't you be uncomfortable if you had two and a half million dollars' worth of life insurance on you, after what has happened?"

But two months later, Joey suggested that they buy two $2 million term life insurance policies, which he said Riggins could provide at a much lower cost in premiums. Bobbie was to be the beneficiary of Joey's policy, and Joey was to be the beneficiary of Bobbie's. Joey did not know that, in October of 1992, Bobbie had written a new will and established a trust, which would leave everything she had at her death not to Joey, as her previous will had stipulated, but to her mother, her sister, her nieces and her nephew.

Bobbie worried that Joey would find out about the new will, and she wondered about Joey's motivation in having her buy life insurance.

She couldn't help thinking, to paraphrase Benjamin Franklin, that, "Two can keep a secret — if one of them is dead."

Bobbie delayed action on the new insurance policies, and they were never put into force. Instead, she took out a different kind of life insurance: She went to a lawyer and asked the lawyer to tip off the cops about her husband.

She may have had additional motives. She had talked with friends about leaving Joey as early as 1989. She told Carla Peoples of Gastonia, the wife of a first cousin of Joey, that Joey had a fierce temper and that, "I had come close to the edge of not being able to take it any more." She told Carla that Randy

Riggins — who was still friendly enough with her to have bought stock in the Caldwells' company — "is really a nice person. I regret leaving him; I think we could have worked things out." She hinted that she was thinking about leaving Joey and remarrying Riggins — who, unlike Joey, was financially successful. Riggins scotched those plans by remarrying in March 1993, but Carla thought that perhaps Bobbie had another prospective new husband in mind by that time.

(It is doubtful that Riggins, at any time between his separation from Bobbie and his second marriage, reciprocated Bobbie's feelings toward him. He told Rick Glaser that he had invested money in the failed Active Woman business, money that he knew he would never realize any return on. He thought his only chance to recoup would be to invest the money — about $10,000 — owed him by Active Woman in the new company, Gymbags. Thus, his 1.1 percent ownership interest in Gymbags did not involve any additional cash outlay. He softened that testimony at trial by saying that his divorce from Barbara had been "amiable," that they had remained good friends even though they saw each other only in business settings, and that he trusted her to the extent that he had not bothered to take her name off their five joint checking and savings accounts until his second wife saw the bank statements and insist that he close the five accounts and open new ones without Bobbie's name. He also testified that he had never mentioned to Bobbie that he had left her name on the accounts — and so she never knew that the money in the accounts was legally available to her.)

In addition to her other possible motives for turning Joey in, Bobbie had feelings of guilt. She had nightmares about the shotgun slayings of the McEacherns. And, some believe, she took a literal guilt trip to Hamlet in late 1991.

"I never saw a picture of Bobbie Caldwell, but a fellow reporter gave me a detailed description of her," said Catherine Monk, a writer for the Richmond County Daily Journal in Rockingham. "I believe it was Bobbie Caldwell who walked into the newsroom one day, came up to my desk, and in a very nervous manner asked me if I could tell her where the McEacherns were buried.

"She wanted to visit their graves, she said."

Bobbie piously told investigators that, despite her fears and feelings of guilt, she waited until after Christmas 1992 to blow the whistle on her husband. "I wanted Joey to have a nice Christmas," she said. "I wanted us to have a nice Thanksgiving and Christmas together."

Perhaps she also waited because she wanted the Christmas gift that Joey gave her that year:

Breast enhancement surgery and facial liposuction.

10.

The proffer from "Client X" said that the murderer had told Client X that he had hit Vela McEachern in the head with a frying pan. The police knew that, but they had never made the information public. There were other details in the proffer that only the murderer or his confidante could have known.

Glaser quickly subpoenaed Bobbie to testify to the grand jury — before contacting "Client X's" attorney with regard to the "Client X" proffer — and she testified in February 1993.

She had testified in an earlier grand jury hearing in February 1992, and that time, she stuck strictly to the story that she and Joey had worked out between them — that they were together throughout the day and night of April 12, 1991, had worked out together at the YMCA, had seen a movie, had shopped at Southpark Mall, and had gone home to watch television.

But in her testimony before the grand jury a year later, she took a different tack. She confirmed that she was Client X, and admitted that she was an accomplice after the fact of the murders.

Later, in open court, during Joey's trial, Bobbie had a five-word explanation for agreeing to testify without a promise of immunity from prosecution.

"He (Glaser) caught me in a lie," she said.

Glaser told her that she had to have been an accessory before the fact, also — and a co-conspirator with her husband in the McEachern murders — if she had, as the proffer had stated, helped to establish Joey's alibi by getting shopping receipts and movie-ticket stubs, trying to show that he had been elsewhere when the murders were committed.

"I hold Bobbie Caldwell just as much to blame for what happened to Maceo and Vela as Joey Caldwell," Naomi Daggs was to say as the 10th anniversary of the murders neared. "The Caldwells' plot had some holes in it that the police and the prosecutors were able to exploit once Bobbie agreed to testify — but if it hadn't been for her testimony, they would have gotten away with it. When I think about all the elements of the plot — the license plate, the gun, the clothing, the tape over the car emblems, even Joey's telling Maceo that Clyde Sullivan had threatened him and, I suspect, advising Maceo to ask the sheriff if Sullivan was a dangerous man, so that Sullivan would become the suspect and not the Caldwells — and you realize that Joey Caldwell was just not smart enough to think all that up. He was not the brightest light in the firmament.

"Joey was the muscle. Bobbie was the brains. Bobbie was the smart one. It was her plan."

Before the grand jury, confronted with Glaser's knowledge of her lying, Bobbie caved in. She decided that her best chance lay in telling the whole truth about the conspiracy and hoping that the judge would be lenient in sentencing her.

. She had already come near to making that decision, when her attorney had caught her in a similar lie. The lawyer had told her that she had three choices: Do nothing, and hope that she would not be subpoenaed and that her problems would all go away; tell the complete truth to a grand jury, with the attorney on hand to advise her; or continue with her original story, and seek other legal representation.

During the three weeks after her grand jury testimony implicated herself and Joey in the McEachern murders, Bobbie stole time away from her husband, meeting at every opportunity with investigators and filling them in on details of the murder plot.

SBI Special Agent Douglas Greene paid a visit to Mac's Gun Shop and located a copy of the Firearms Transaction Report that Joey, as "Arthur Scott," had filled out in purchasing the gun. The report contained a fictitious address, on a "Fitsjerral" Street — evidently Joey's creative misspelling of "Fitzgerald." In a later interview with Joey, Greene asked him to write the word "Fitzgerald." "He asked me how to spell it," Greene recounted, "and I said to spell it like he thought it should be spelled. He spelled it 'Fitsjarrel.' "

"Once," Naomi Daggs recalled, "Maceo handed me something that Joey Caldwell had written — some business paper or other — and asked me to type it. I looked at it, and it was riddled with misspellings. The man was nearly illiterate. I pointed out to Maceo that he was doing business with an illiterate man, but he just laughed and said, 'In a few years we'll all be millionaires, and then it won't matter that he can't spell.' I think it's ironic that Caldwell's bad spelling is one of the things that tripped him up."

The handwriting on the gun form matched samples of Joey's handwriting that Bobbie had surreptitiously gathered from Joey, according to SBI Special Agent David C. Dunn, a documents examiner in the SBI Crime Laboratory in Raleigh.

Also at Mac's Gun Shop, the agents found boxes of shells consistent with the type of plastic wadding and shreds of paper wrapping that forensics specialists had found at the murder scene. The shells were of a type, said Thomas Trochum of the SBI Crime Lab, that had not been manufactured for more than 20 years. Their age, he said, made it probable that they had become misshapen, possibly causing the unusual shot pattern noted in the murders.

Bobbie also took investigators to a construction site on Old Dowd Road in Charlotte, where, she said, Joey had stolen the concrete block that he placed in Vela McEachern's driveway on the night of April 10, 1991 — hoping that, when Maceo arrived home, he would get out of his car to move the block and Joey could shoot him from ambush. On March 5, 1993, three concrete blocks from the building site were delivered to the SBI Crime Lab, where forensic specialist

W.E. Pearce matched soil and "mineralogical materials" clinging to the rough surface of the blocks with similar materials on the block that Hamlet police had retrieved from the McEachern lawn. Pearce determined that the soil on all four blocks, and the sand materials used in the mortar mix, were "close matches," although he could not be certain that all four had ever been at the same location.

11.

Jim Thomas, an investigator with the Hamlet Police Department, was a tall, lanky man who shared Terry Moore's passion for Civil War memorabilia. Often, during shared lunches or in the police station on relatively quiet days, he and Moore would page through catalogs of memorabilia, deciding which items they could afford to buy on their policemen's salaries, and sometimes pooling their money to buy collections of buttons or minie balls which they would divide between them.

Thomas had been a police officer for nearly twenty years — nearly as long as Moore — and had once been the police chief in the nearby town of Ellerbe, which, with a population less than 1,000, could afford to pay only one officer and some auxiliary officers. Thomas liked the work, but he moved to the Hamlet Police Department when the opportunity came because the benefits were better, the pay was higher, the hours were more regular, and he would have more time to spend with his teen-aged son, Eddie. Thomas's first marriage had broken up years before — "Police work and family life are often not a good combination," he would say — but he never shirked his duties as a father, paying child support regularly and on time and taking every opportunity to spend time with Eddie.

He did not like to be sent on out-of-town assignments.

But in late February of 1993, Thomas agreed to go to Belmont and search through the kudzu-infested ravine below the Harris Teeter store for the electronic equipment that Bobbie said Joey had thrown there on April 13, 1991.

He spent most of the day at the job, slogging through the kudzu swinging a bush hog, occasionally getting on hands and knees and digging at the soil with his fingers. He came up with beer cans, Wendy's hamburger wrappers, an assortment of other trash, but no electronic equipment.

He repeated the trip several days later, getting directions from Bobbie as to her recollection of where Joey had thrown the devices. After several hours of swinging the bush hog and digging under the kudzu, he found several weathered and rusted pieces of electronic equipment that Bobbie identified as the items Joey had tossed into the ravine. The electronic equipment did not mean much in itself, but it was further evidence that Bobbie was now telling the truth to the investigators.

IX.

ARREST AND TRIAL

1.

The net around Joey Caldwell was growing tighter, but investigators were not satisfied. They hoped to get a tape recording of Joey talking about the murder with his wife.

On the morning of March 11, 1993, Bobbie met with Janie Swain, a female agent from the Fayetteville SBI office. Swain fitted her with a recording device — what police call "a wire" — that was invisible underneath her clothing. At the same time, SBI Special Agent Bill Lane gave Joey a letter informing him that he was a prime suspect in the federal grand jury investigation. They figured that would jolt Joey into discussing the crime with his wife.

When Bobbie returned home, she and Joey drove to a Chili's Grill and Bar in a shopping center in Gastonia for lunch. On the one-hour, 13-minute tape of their drive and their lunch together, their voices mingle with engine noises and the conversations of the restaurant crowd — but most of what they said is clearly audible.

Joey was reticent about the murders. He spoke about the behavior of the couple's cocker spaniels, about friends, about business plans.

But Bobbie kept steering the conversation back to the murders.

"You know the stuff that you had with you?" she said.

"Yeah."

"What did you do with it?"

"I don't know what stuff you're talking about."

"You know, the gun and the clothes —"

"Scattered all over the place."

She asked him, "How about the house, shells or —"

"Baby," he interjected, "if they found the shells, they wouldn't do anything with them. But there wasn't — there weren't. If there was, they would have already come and seen me."

"Could the investigators find out about (you) buying the shotgun?"Bobbie asked.

"I dunno," Joey said. "I don't see how ... I can't see how — I told nobody."

"Could anyone have seen (Joey) coming out of the McEachern house?" she asked.

"No. If they had, they would've — they would've done it a long time ago," Joey said. "They must have something, though. They've got to have something, or they wouldn't tell me that I'm a target."

Joey talked twice on the tape about the possibility of committing suicide if he were caught. "I couldn't do that," Bobbie told him. "That's not an option for me."

"When I started," Joey said, "I made the decision to take the consequences. ... My only concern about this whole thing is that it doesn't come back on you."

"Insurance won't pay off on suicide," Bobbie said. Although she knew that SBI agents were listening and that Joey's arrest was probably imminent, she couldn't help voicing her financial concerns.

"We don't have insurance," Joey said.

"In a month we will."

At one point during the meal Bobbie excused herself and visited the women's restroom, where Janie Swain was waiting. "Can you hear us?" she asked. "Is the recorder working?"

"You're both coming in loud and clear," Swain assured her.

When Bobbie returned to the table, Joey began speaking of the possibility that he would be arrested, and he hinted again that he might commit suicide.

"I'll never go back to the door without my gun," he said. "It's not like I'm willing to go through a trial and all that."

Lane and other agents arrested Joey as he and Bobbie stepped out of the restaurant.

A lot of people had wanted to be in on the arrest. Sixteen law officers — local, state, and federal — were present in the Chili's parking lot.

2.

Joey was indicted on fifty-nine federal counts — weapons violations (e.g., transporting a weapon across state lines to commit a felony), mail fraud (in his insurance claims), witness tampering (agents suspected that he had attempted to influence Bobbie's grand jury testimony), and money laundering. One of the mail fraud counts was later dropped on a technicality.

From the time of his arrest until his nine-day federal trial in Greensboro ended on Sept. 1, 1993, Joey was confined in the High Point Jail, the nearest lockup to the federal courthouse in Greensboro where his trial was to be held.

He kept in shape by doing 500 push-ups a day, but deprived of his regular weightlifting workouts, he slimmed down. By the time his trial began in late August, he no longer looked like a former state karate champion; he looked pale and almost frail in comparison with his bulky frame a few months earlier.

He hired Charlotte attorney Lawrence W. "Larry" Hewitt to represent him in court. He kept up an optimistic front with friends and relatives, saying that he never doubted that he would be found not guilty.

He also said he had found Jesus and discovered a newfound peace in his life. But on the witness stand during his trial, he lied.

3.

Joey could not be tried for murder, because Bobbie could not testify against him in a state court unless he waived the "spousal privilege," which he naturally had no intention of doing. But the prosecution in the federal case against him would have to prove that Joey committed the murders in order to prove the fraud, weapons and money-laundering charges. It would be a tricky case to prosecute.

Personnel in the U.S. Attorney's office, headed by Assistant U.S. Attorney Rick Glaser, would spend the months before trial going over evidence, gathering the extensive documentation required to prove their case, preparing and trying out various approaches to the presentation of evidence, interviewing witnesses, issuing subpoenas — all in an effort to present at trial what Glaser hoped would be a seamless case against Joey.

The Hamlet Police Department had a considerable role in the preparation. Its officers put Glaser's office in touch with witnesses, gathered up the physical evidence and shipped it off to Greensboro to be used as trial exhibits, and went over the department's mammoth file of notes and reports on the investigation in order to be prepared to testify accurately if called to the stand.

But even as the department's workload increased with trial preparation, Chief Terry Moore said, "We couldn't just let all our bicycle thefts go. We still had to investigate the day-to-day crimes, testify in court, file reports, do all the things we ordinarily did."

Another shocking murder occurred in Hamlet on April 5, 1993. Larry Brown Jr., the 28-year-old owner and operator of the Sandhill Jewelry & Pawn Shop on U.S. Highway 74 West, was shot and killed in the course of an armed robbery at his store.

Relying on witness descriptions of the shooter and the car in which the robbers drove out of town, the police quickly cleared the case, arresting three young Bennettsville, South Carolina, men ranging in age from 15 to 24 and charging them with armed robbery and murder.

Now the police had three new murder trials to prepare for. But they persevered in their preparations for the Caldwell trial.

4.

Joey's trial began in U.S. District Court in Greensboro, North Carolina, 65 miles north of Hamlet, on Monday, August 20, 1993. Presiding was Judge William L. Osteen, Sr., a gray-haired man with a large and imposing court presence, who had suffered few reversals at the hands of appellate courts during a long and distinguished career on the state and federal benches.

Jury selection went surprisingly quickly, and witnesses began to take the stand on the first day of the trial.

Early witnesses for the prosecution gave brief testimony calculated to put Joey at the murder scene. Margie Bohannon testified that she had seen a car with an Ontario license plate near the McEacherns' driveway, as did Hughes Webster and Callie Ellison. Bohannon and Webster described a man standing near the car — about 5 feet, 10 inches tall, with long, bushy or curly, sand-colored hair, wearing casual clothing. Ellison said he had noticed that the car had tape across its brand-name symbols.

Chris Cox told the jury what Vela McEachern had told him on April 12 about the concrete block in her driveway. His testimony later proved to be crucial to the prosecution's case.

5.

Glaser put his key witness, Bobbie Caldwell, on the stand next. Slight, with blonde hair trimmed short, she looked prim in a white blouse buttoned to the neck, a white sweater, a pleated gray skirt, modest gold earrings and spectacles.

Joey watched her intently throughout her testimony, showing no emotion, occasionally taking notes. He scribbled madly on his yellow legal pad when she testified that she had stayed with him through 1992 because she wanted him to have "a nice Christmas." He wore a light gray suit, a blue shirt with a rumpled collar, and a conservative striped tie. His black hair, cut short, was graying at the sides.

Bobbie's testimony consumed the remainder of the first day of the trial and all the second day. She repeated for the jury all that she had told SBI agents, laying out the plot to kill Maceo, the purchase of the gun, the thefts of the license plate and cinder block, her actions on the night of the murders, and what Joey had told her about shooting the McEacherns. She attempted to tell about Joey's taking the lie-detector test under the influence of drugs, but defense attorney

Larry Hewitt objected and Osteen had that part of the testimony stricken from the official trial record.

Glaser completed his questioning of Bobbie by asking: "Ms. Caldwell, have any promises, representations, or any agreements been made with the United States, as far as what is going to happen to you or what has happened to you up to now?"

"No, there isn't," Bobbie answered.

"Why are you testifying?" Glaser asked.

"Because the truth needed to be told. I was caught in a lie, and it needed to be told."

"Do you hope that your testifying may help you?"

"Sure."

Bobbie was telling the truth. Prosecutors had cut no deals for her, and she had not been promised immunity from prosecution for her own part in the murders. But there was more to her decision to testify than her feeling that "the truth needed to be told." She had been thinking about leaving Joey for some time, and after he began to press her about buying life insurance, she feared for her life if he were to remain free.

Hewitt bored in hard on the issue of immunity as he opened his cross-examination of Bobbie:

Q. Ms. Caldwell, your husband, you're aware, is charged in a 59-count bill of indictment in this court, with mail fraud, money laundering, and the so-called gun charges, transportation and use of firearms, and intimidating or influencing a witness charge. You're aware of those charges, are you not?

A. I don't know how many counts there are.

Q. Well, you're not charged in that bill of indictment, are you? You are not charged in that bill of indictment, are you?

A. No.

Q. You are not charged with anything, are you?

A. No

Q. In fact, you walk in and out of this court free? I mean, you are not under any restraint or arrest?

A. No.

Q. In fact, you are employed in the Charlotte/Mecklenburg school system, are you not?

A. Yes, sir.

Q. Signed a one-year contract with them?

A. Yes, sir.

Q. You hope to complete that contract, don't you?

A. I hope so.

Q. You certainly went in with the expectation of completing that?

A. I hope so.

Q. There are no charges pending against you in any jurisdiction arising out of the death of Maceo McEachern, are there?

A. Not right now.

Q. But today, as you sit here, there are no charges?

A. No.

Q. And you have never been arrested by the federal authorities in conjunction with the charges for which your husband stands charged, and for which you are testifying against him today, have you?

A. No, sir.

Q. And you don't expect to ever be arrested, do you, or charged?

A. Yes, sir.

Q. In the federal jurisdiction?

A. I expect that, yes.

Q. Ms. Caldwell, you have — it has been made aware to you, either directly or indirectly, that you are not going to be charged or suffer any consequences in the federal jurisdiction, that is, the federal court system, as a result of these charges brought against your husband; isn't that correct?

A. Say that again.

Q. I am saying that you understand that nobody is going to bring any charges against you in the federal jurisdiction arising out of the death of Maceo McEachern, don't you?

A. No, sir.

Q. You understand that, don't you?

A. No. I don't have any guarantee to that.

Q. Well, you understand if you come in this courtroom and testify —

MR. GLASER: Asked and answered, your honor.

THE COURT: Overruled.

Q. You understand if you come in this courtroom and testify, as you have done yesterday and today, that you're going to be granted immunity and not going to be prosecuted, don't you, in the federal jurisdiction?

A. No, sir.

Q. You don't understand that?

A. No, sir.

Q. Well, did anybody talk to you, any federal prosecutors or anybody out of the Justice Department talk to you about being charged in the same bill of indictment with Joey Caldwell, and why you were not? Was anything discussed about that subject?

A. I'm sorry. You lost me again.

Q. My question simply to you is, have you had any discussion with any of the prosecutors, or anybody else with the federal government, about why you were not charged in the federal indictment that we're trying this case about right now?

A. No. I haven't had any discussion with them at all concerning that.

Q. Well, you have sat up there, as I have heard your testimony yesterday and today, and admitted that you were a co-conspirator in a murder?

A. With my husband, yes.

Q. And some other matters: mail fraud, money laundering, and all that. And you haven't been charged with any of that, correct?

A. I have not been charged; that's correct.

Q. Well, if you expect to go — have something happen to you by way of being charged, or something like that, why did you sign a one-year contract with the Charlotte/Mecklenburg school system?

MR. GLASER: Objection, your honor.

THE COURT: Overruled.

THE WITNESS: I was told that I needed to continue with my life, until the time that an action was taken.

Q. Now, the bottom line, Ms. Caldwell, you expect to get off that witness stand either this afternoon or tomorrow morning, and walk out of this courtroom, and not be back in a federal court again; isn't that true? Isn't that what you expect?

A. No, sir.

Q. You don't expect that?

A. No, sir.

Q. Sure is what you hope, isn't it?

A. Sure, it is.

Q. And you are willing to come in here and testify, to whatever it takes from your perspective, to assure that that hope becomes a reality, aren't you?

A. You need to say that again.

Q. I am simply saying, your ability to come in here and testify against your husband, whom you said you loved on that tape, right before you turned him in to be arrested — you are willing to come in here and testify, and say whatever you need to say, so that you can walk out of this courtroom and not have to come back here, aren't you?

A. I am still not sure —

Q. I am simply saying, you are willing to testify to almost anything to get your neck out of the noose?

A. That's not true.

Hewitt's aim had been to discredit Bobbie in the eyes of the jury. And, he was to learn later, he had succeeded — in the eyes of at least one juror.

6.

On the second day of her testimony, over the objections of Hewitt, Osteen ruled that the tape of the Caldwells' March 11 conversation could be played for the jury.

It was a devastating defeat for the defense. Out of the presence of the jury, Hewitt had argued at length that the tape should not be played. "(I)t is our position," he told Osteen, "that the conspiracy, if such a thing existed, or the participation on the part of this witness(,) certainly ceased and terminated prior to any conversation on this tape. Therefore, she was not a participant in a crime at that time. She was functioning as a government agent, or arm of the government, and we would contend at that point the privilege [of confidential communication] comes back into play, and would ask that that tape be suppressed, and that those conversations do fall under the protection of confidential communication."

After a recess, during which Osteen studied a brief that Glaser had written in support of playing the tape, Osteen said: "I am reasonably convinced that once a husband and wife begin to talk about criminal activity, and participate in plans for criminal activity, that any conversations thereafter about it, whether the criminal activity is still going on or not going on, is not a violation of the privilege."

After Hewitt's associate Richard Fennell offered another argument to suppress the tape, Osteen said: "I have a hard time understanding how you can waive the privilege by talking about criminal activity, and then enforce the privilege again when you continue to talk about it after the parties have been a participant."

Hewitt insisted on a "continuing" or "blanket" objection to the playing of the tape, and Osteen granted him his objection. Hewitt reasoned that the continuing objection might be crucial if Joey were to be convicted. Hewitt would then prepare an appeal on grounds that the tape should not have been played in the jury's presence.

Osteen ordered the jury brought back into the courtroom, and Bobbie's testimony resumed.

The next morning, after Bobbie concluded her testimony, Osteen ordered a clerk to distribute transcripts of the tape to members of the jury and to the prosecution and defense attorneys. He instructed the jury that, while they might follow the conversation on the tape by looking at the transcripts, they should rely on their own understanding of the words they heard on the tape rather than the typed transcripts.

The tape was played for the jury.

The combination of Bobbie's testimony and the tape was devastating for Joey. When Osteen allowed the tape to be played, Hewitt must have known that his client didn't have a chance of acquittal. The best Hewitt could hope for would be a hung jury and a second trial — in which, perhaps, the ruling on the tape might go the other way — or a conviction and an appeal. An appeals court, he reasoned, might order a new trial, *sans* tape.

7.

The feisty Glaser brought a parade of other witnesses to the stand — police officers, SBI agents, forensic scientists, and an expert on money laundering from the Internal Revenue Service — to weave together the circumstantial evidence that Bobbie's confessions had led investigators to discover.

Thomas Trochum of the SBI Lab told the jury that the McEacherns had been shot with "00" or "0" buckshot — either nine or twelve pellets per shell, capable of doing tremendous damage to tissue. Both, he said, were shot from a distance of no more than four feet. He explained about the wadding and paper shreds found in the McEacherns' den, which showed that the shotgun shells were of a type that had not been manufactured for decades. But under cross-examination from Hewitt, he said that he would not be able, from the evidence at the scene, to identify the gun(s) that had been used in the shootings or to establish how many guns there had been.

SBI Special Agent Leroy Allen walked the jury through the agents' visit to the Caldwells' house on April 13, 1991. He told of locating the "cement cinderblocks" at the construction site on Old Dowd Road, and said that the blocks had been delivered to that location in September 1990.

Glaser entered the Caldwells' cellular telephone bill from January 1991 into evidence, and Allen testified that a call to Mac's Gun Shop was on the bill.

8.

SBI Special Agent Douglas Greene told the jury about finding the "Firearms Transaction Report" at Mac's Gun Shop and about Joey's misspellings of the name "Fitzgerald."

Glaser at this point attempted to introduce into evidence the form that Joey, as "Arthur Scott," had filled out at Mac's Gun Shop. Hewitt objected, and Osteen would not allow the form as evidence unless Bobbie returned to testify that the form appeared to her to be in Joey's handwriting. Glaser agreed to subpoena Bobbie, and Osteen sent bailiffs to the school where she was teaching that day to bring her immediately to the courtroom. Her appearance, when she arrived in court, presented a stark contrast to her appearance on the first two days of the trial. This time, she was wearing a tight, mustard-colored pullover sweater and a tight dress with a slit up the side — an unusual outfit, to say the least, for a middle-school teacher at work, and one that showed all too clearly the success of her recent breast enhancement surgery. She wore contact lenses rather than spectacles, and she had replaced her tasteful earrings with large gold hoops.

SBI Special Agent Bill Lane, who sat at the prosecution table throughout the trial, took the stand only briefly. Under questioning by Assistant U.S. Attorney Sandra J. Hairston, Lane attempted to testify about the Joey Caldwell handwriting exemplars that Bobbie had obtained from business files that she kept at home. Osteen sustained Hewitt's objection that the prosecution had laid "no basis" for the introduction of this evidence. Glaser decided not to bring to the stand a handwriting expert that he had hoped would testify, since he felt sure that Hewitt would make a similar objection and Osteen would sustain it.

Wendell Wells, M.D., Maceo's personal physician, told the court that in the weeks prior to the murders, Randy Riggins was "frantic" to receive the information from him about Maceo's follow-up blood-pressure readings.

9.

Riggins testified about the Caldwells' insurance history, the mammoth amounts of life insurance they had taken out. He also testified about Maceo's key man policies and put a different twist on Wells' testimony by saying that Wells was "slow to respond" to his inquiries.

He testified that Bobbie had been "aggressive" in pressuring him to get the key man policies into force.

And he revealed something that Joey and Bobbie had apparently not known: They had thought that the key man policies, though dated April 14, 1991, had gone into effect when Bobbie picked them up — the Great West policy on April 4, the Sun Life policy on April 10. Actually, he said, both policies had gone into effect on April 4, the day Bobbie gave Riggins checks for the initial premium payments.

10.

Hamlet police officer Jim Thomas told the jury about finding the electronic equipment in the ravine below Harris Teeter in Belmont. "We didn't find anything, the first time," he said. "The second time, in March 1993, Barbara Caldwell went with us and gave directions, and we found some of the devices." Under cross-examination, Thomas said that he found other discarded electronic equipment, including an abandoned television set, in the search area.

W.E. Pearce of the SBI Lab testified that the concrete blocks the SBI had retrieved from the Old Dowd Road construction site were a "close match" with the block found in the McEacherns' yard. But Hewitt got him to admit that the soil on the block in Hamlet appeared to be "somewhat different" from the soil on the other blocks, and that the concrete blocks were of a "generic" type, not greatly different from other concrete blocks manufactured at other places and at other times.

11.

Bobbie was still in the courtroom, and Glaser made another attempt to enter Joey's handwriting samples into evidence. This time, Osteen overruled Hewitt's objections, and Bobbie took the stand and identified some of the samples as being in Joey's handwriting.

Hewitt desperately tried to derail Glaser's line of questioning. The handwriting identification was a vital element of the weapons charges against Joey. And if Glaser could not establish that Joey had bought the weapon, he would have a more difficult time proving that Joey was the murderer — a proof on which the whole case against Joey depended. Hewitt objected repeatedly to Glaser's questions, questioning whether Bobbie had the expertise to identify her husband's handwriting. Osteen overruled the objections, and Glaser plowed forward.

Then Hewitt made a valiant attempt to confuse both Bobbie and the prosecution by insisting that the handwriting exemplars be divided into categories. Some of the handwriting samples were more than one page long, and some of the pages in those samples were typed and had no handwriting on them. Hewitt demanded that these pages be placed in a separate pile. Then he demanded that other distinctions be made — pages on which only Joey's signature appeared, pages that Bobbie had seen her husband write, pages that she had not seen him write but believed that he had written, pages that she was unsure of. The pages were placed in separate piles, and a court clerk was kept busy stapling some of the papers together and putting paper clips on others. Glaser got into the act by suggesting that the clerk label the various categories of papers with colored tabs so that they could be found more easily, and suggesting that the defense exhibit consisting of the papers be sub-labeled "A," "B," "C," and "D." The whole process took up the better part of an hour — but in the end, Glaser was able to get the testimony he needed on the record.

Glaser then walked Bobbie through the entire form that Joey had filled out in Mac's Gun Shop, pointing to each line of the form and asking whether she had seen Joey write on that line. In all cases, except for the lines that were left blank and one that was left for the gun shop's clerk to fill in, Bobbie said that Joey had done the writing and that she had seen him do it.

Lane took the stand again to establish the "chain of possession" of the handwriting samples, saying that he had received them from Bobbie and had mailed them to SBI documents examiner David C. Dunn. Then Dunn took the stand to testify that he was "virtually certain" that the exemplars obtained by Bobbie matched the handwriting of the Firearms Transaction Report filled out by "Arthur Scott" at Mac's Gun Shop.

12.

Charlotte attorney Charles Simmons, who had represented the Caldwells in the sale of the Pro-Formance formula and trademark to Maceo's company Ventures, Inc., was on the stand for a lengthy period, filling the jury in on the tangled financial history of Gymbags and the negotiations among the Caldwells, Clyde Sullivan, and Maceo.

"Mr. Simmons," Glaser asked, "did you — after the death of Maceo McEachern, were you contacted by Joey Caldwell and Bobby Caldwell?"

"At some point, yes."

"What, if anything, did they relate to you regarding the collection of the insurance policy on Maceo McEachern?"

"They asked that we pursue the Gymbags' claims against both Sun Life and Great West."

"Do you recall how soon after the death they contacted you all (Simmons' law firm) to do that?"

"It was not immediately. But not a tremendous amount of time passed."

The Internal Revenue Service, apprised of the insurance payouts, advised Simmons of the Caldwells' tax debt, he testified. Glaser asked him how often, after the IRS notification, the Caldwells had contacted him about collecting the insurance proceeds.

"Fairly frequently," Simmons said. "(We) talked about that, as well as we were trying to put together a list of the amounts that all of their creditors were owed. So, we were talking about money for a lot of different reasons."

"And you were talking to both Joey Caldwell and Bobby Caldwell about these things?"

"Yes."

Simmons testified that the Caldwells received two life insurance checks in the amounts of $1,553,355 and $514,440. Using copies of bank statements, deposit slips and debit advises, he traced the Caldwells' deposits of the money into various bank accounts and a few major disbursements, primarily to pay dividends to various stockholders in Gymbags and debts that the Caldwells had owed from previous business ventures. Glaser was laying the groundwork for later, more detailed testimony about the Caldwells' disbursements — which he hoped to use to prove the charges of money laundering.

As Hewitt began to cross-examine Simmons, a tremendous clap of thunder rattled the windows of the courtroom.

"Ladies and gentlemen of the jury," Judge Osteen said as thunder continued to rumble, "there seems to be some indication from a voice greater than the courtroom that we maybe ought to take a break about now. And I believe we will do that, and see if we can get over a little of this storm, so you can concentrate on what we're hearing here."

After the break, Simmons testified about the negotiations between the Caldwells and Clyde Sullivan after Maceo's death. Sullivan had pressed the Caldwells hard to make a cash settlement in his countersuit against them over Sullivan's earlier attempt to buy distribution rights for Pro-Formance. With Maceo no longer available as a witness for Joey in his lawsuit, the case was a lost cause for the Caldwells. But Sullivan was demanding a settlement of $250,000 — a sizable sum even for a couple who had just received two million dollars in insurance proceeds, especially considering the number and amounts of their debts.

"I believe that insurance funds were the source of the payment to the Sullivans," Simmons said, "so I would imagine settlement took place after payment of one or both of those insurance policies."

Hewitt refreshed Simmons' memory by showing him a letter, dated August 5, 1991, from Simmons's law partner Sam Woodard to Jackson Steele at the Petree Stockton law firm. "Who did Mr. Steele represent, if you know?" Hewitt asked.

"I believe he was the last in the line of Clyde Sullivan's attorneys," Simmons replied. (An earlier attorney for Sullivan in the settlement negotiations had been former North Carolina Governor Jim Holshouser, who headed a prestigious law firm in Pinehurst and Southern Pines.)

Hewitt asked Simmons to tell the jury "the substance of this letter."

"In it," Simmons said, "Sam states that 'Faison Hicks and I completed another meeting with the board of directors of Gymbags. The board rejected your client's second settlement offer of $250,000.' It says, 'We have advised them that your clients have under consideration a settlement counteroffer of Gymbags of $100,000. I apologize again for having to tell you our client insists settlement discussions have to be concluded promptly, or they will withdraw the $100,000 settlement offer and give a drop-dead time here of 10 a.m. tomorrow morning, Tuesday, August 6th."

The phrase "drop-dead time" took on new resonance, in light of Bobbie's earlier testimony that she and Joey had initially planned to kill Clyde Sullivan.

Hewitt plowed ahead: "Mr. Simmons, is it your recollection that the — both the litigation and negotiations back and forth to resolve this stock situation between the Sullivans, Clyde Sullivan and his family, and Joey Caldwell and Gymbags, was somewhat bitter and acrimonious?"

"Yes, I would say so."

(The eventual settlement was for $175,000.)

Hewitt's line of questioning was disingenuous, calling attention as it did to his client's shaky financial situation even after the insurance payouts. But Hewitt, like Glaser, was laying groundwork — in this case, for a defense scenario suggesting that the hard-bargaining Sullivan, not Joey, could have been the murderer.

Glaser, however, sensed an opening, and he bore in on redirect, asking: "Mr. Simmons, at the time of the sale of the company, what was the — on February 15th, 1991 — what was the financial health of Gymbags, Inc., at the time that it sold the Pro-Formance formula and trademark?"

"I believe they had serious cash-flow problems," Simmons said. "And the balance sheet is referenced in one of these letters. It indicates a negative net worth of $14,000, and a fair amount was owed to creditors. We prepared a schedule of all of the amounts owed, and tried to negotiate down the amounts we paid to some of those creditors."

"So, even after the sale of the company, it stayed in a precarious financial condition?"

"Yes. They received a payment up front from Venture Distributors, and then would receive royalties over time, which, in the beginning, were not sufficient to satisfy the — all of the creditors."

13.

Adrian Barnett, group manager of the Criminal Investigations Division of the IRS office in Greensboro, told the jury that he had carefully traced the Caldwells' financial transactions since receiving the insurance checks. He told of the various bank deposits, withdrawals, and major purchases the Caldwells made over the two-year period in which they went through the $2 million in insurance proceeds.

Barnett's testimony took most of an afternoon. After he stepped down from the witness stand, Glaser announced that the prosecution was resting its case.

14.

Clyde Sullivan had been listed as a witness for the prosecution, but Glaser did not call him. That was good strategy on Glaser's part, for if Sullivan had taken the stand, Hewitt might have had the chance during cross-examination to establish that Sullivan had a violent background. That would have better enabled him to frame an alternative theory of the murders: that Sullivan had hired someone to kill the McEacherns, in order to keep Maceo from testifying against him in the hearing on Joey's lawsuit.

Hewitt, of course, could still have called Sullivan to the stand as a defense witness — but he knew that if he had done so, Osteen would not have allowed him to impugn his own witness. Calling Sullivan to the stand would only have weakened what Hewitt must have realized was an already weak case.

15.

After the prosecution rested, Richard Fennell entered a complex defense motion for directed acquittal. He argued that the mail fraud charges were not legitimate because the letters from Gymbags to Clyde Sullivan were required by law and therefore "were not caused by Joey Caldwell;" that mailing Maceo's death certificate to the insurance companies "did not further any criminal scheme;" and that Riggins and Simmons, not Joey, were the agents who mailed Wendell Wells requests for Maceo's medical history.

Fennell asked that the court throw out the witness tampering charge because there had been no testimony to the effect that Joey had tried to persuade Bobbie to lie to the grand jury in February 1993. "At that time," Fennell said, "by her own testimony, she was still a willing participant, and she lied on her own." (Actually, Bobbie had testified that she had talked with Joey about "keeping the same story that we had before" — the same story that she had told the grand jury in October 1992.)

The 50 charges of money laundering should be dismissed, Fennell argued, because in order to find Joey guilty of money laundering the prosecution must prove that the funds derived "from a specific unlawful activity." But the funds, he argued, derived "from actions taken after the murder."

Osteen denied all parts of Fennell's motion.

16.

Hewitt tried manfully to counter the prosecution's case. In Joey's defense, he called to the stand relatives — including Joey's mother and father — friends, and neighbors of the Caldwells, all of whose testimony was calculated to shed doubt on Bobbie's motives and truthfulness.

Testimony by the first three defense witnesses was designed to cast doubt on Bobbie's testimony that Joey had been away from home on the night the murders were committed. But the die was cast by Bobby Peoples, Jr.'s testimony, and it was a disaster for the defense.

Peoples, a first cousin of Joey, testified that he had called Joey from a bowling alley at about 9 p.m. on April 12, 1991, to tell Joey about a quarrel that Peoples had had with his son that afternoon and to ask Joey's advice on dealing with the boy. He placed the call to Joey's home, he said.

He admitted that, when interviewed by SBI agents on February 4, 1992, he did not tell them about the phone call. "I didn't remember it then," he said, "but I later remembered the date because it was the weekend of a shag dancing function I had planned to attend."

Glaser bore in on Peoples in cross-examination, getting him to admit that, around the time of the McEachern murders, Peoples had had a drinking problem — "so bad I had to put myself into the hospital."

"When did you remember making that phone call?" Glaser asked.

"After I did research," Peoples said.

"When was that?" Glaser asked.

"After Joey was arrested. Is that what you want to hear?" Peoples responded.

"Why didn't you tell the SBI after you remembered?" Glaser asked.

"Because of Mr. Lane — because Mr. Lane had a vendetta against Joey Caldwell.'

Glaser asked if Peoples had been drinking on the night he telephoned Joey from the bowling alley. Peoples said he had drunk "one beer — two beers."

"Was it one, or two?" Glaser asked.

"Maybe three."

"Maybe five or six?"

"Put what figure you want to put," Peoples retorted.

Osteen excused the jury and instructed Peoples, "You must answer the questions with the facts as you remember those facts to be. It's not your job to make 'smart' remarks or 'cute' remarks. I do not want you sparring with the attorneys in this case."

The jury was recalled. Glaser asked Peoples what he knew about a "vendetta" against Joey by SBI Agent Lane. "What I know is from Joey and Bobbie's statements about remarks made by Lane. I wasn't there," Peoples said.

Glaser returned to the question of how many beers Peoples had consumed before he made the telephone call to Joey.

"Could it have been six beers?"

"Yes, sir."

"Ten?"

"Yes, sir."

"Twenty?"

"No, sir."

"No further questions."

Hewitt wisely chose not to pursue re-direct examination.

17.

The next witness was Joyce Southard, Joey's mother, who had remarried and was living in Starke, Florida, working as a nurse assistant in a retirement home. She testified that, on April 12, 1991, she had called Joey between 8:30 and 9 p.m. from a convenience store about one and one-half miles from her home. "My telephone cord was broken, and I couldn't use my phone," she said. She added that she didn't charge the call to her own phone, and so the call would not be reflected on her phone bill.

"I called Joey," Joyce Southard said, "to borrow $2,000 for my daughter for a couple of weeks. ... I remember (the date) because my granddaughter's birthday was April 19, and that was the week before her birthday. School was out, and she (the granddaughter) had come down on Friday evening. We had cake and ice cream."

Again, with Joyce Southard, Glaser's cross-examination was effective.

"You called your son again that weekend?" he asked.

"Only on the Friday night. ... We talked for two or three minutes."

Glaser entered into evidence Joyce Southard's telephone bill for April 1991 and reminded her that it contained a billing for a six-minute call made on Sunday, April 14, 1991, to Joey in Belmont.

He asked her when she remembered making the April 12 call.

"I remembered it after Joey reminded me — I remembered the phone call; he just refreshed my memory."

Glaser asked when Joey had "refreshed her memory."

"I have no idea."

"Was it in connection with this trial?"

"No, sir — I mean, not to my knowledge."

"Was it in connection with the investigation?"

"No."

"Did he ask you to call anybody (and tell them about the call)?"

"No."

18.

Hewitt called Floy Dean Caldwell of Gastonia, Joey's father, to the stand.

The elder Caldwell worked in a Western Auto appliance store, and he testified that he had ordered a leaf blower for his son and that the store received the leaf blower on April 10, 1991. That was the day that, according to Bobbie's testimony, Joey had stayed in Hamlet until after midnight, waiting for Maceo to come home and get out of his car to remove the concrete block from his driveway.

Dean Caldwell testified that he had called Joey at home about 4:30 p.m. on April 10 to tell him the leaf blower had arrived. "He wasn't there. I called him (from home) between 7:30 and 8 o'clock that night and told him."

On cross-examination, Dean Caldwell said he had never told any law enforcement agents about the telephone call — "only my son's lawyer."

(On re-direct, he said no SBI agents had ever interviewed him.)

Dean had a copy of his phone bill for the month, showing that he made a call to Joey's home on April 10. "He remembered talking to me," Dean said, "and I remembered it as well. That's why I got this record out of my personal file."

Dean Caldwell's testimony was the strongest of the three "alibi" witnesses, and it became stronger when his wife, Linda, took the stand to corroborate his testimony. "It was just getting dark" at the time Dean made the call from home, she recalled.

Their testimony left open the question of when, on April 10, Joey had left home to go to Hamlet. Bobbie had never said.

Given that Dean Caldwell's testimony was truthful, it would be wrong to accuse Bobby Peoples and Joyce Southard of lying on the witness stand.

More likely, Joey had, in his mother's words, "refreshed their memories" about calls they had, in fact, made on other dates, impressing on them the belief that they made the calls on April 12. It is significant that neither call was made from a home telephone, and that billing records could not establish whether they had been made on the dates the witnesses said they were made.

19.

Bobby Peoples, Jr.'s wife Carla testified that she cleaned the Caldwells' house twice a week. Once, she said, she spotted a half-inch-thick sheaf of $100 bills in a laundry hamper. She asked Bobbie about the money, she said, and Bobbie told her that she and Joey owed $300,000 and were withdrawing cash and keeping it hidden in various places so that debtors could not garnishee it from their bank accounts.

Carla Peoples said Bobbie had told her that the Caldwells had $50,000 hidden in the engine compartment of their boat, $50,000 in the laundry hamper, $50,000 in a freezer, an $10,000 in a green First Union National Bank bag in Joey's desk at home.

"In February (1993), she said she would be financially secure in one year," Carla said. "She loved Joey, but (she said) if she ever got rid of him, she'd never do that again. ... She was looking out of the window. I asked her, 'Is something wrong?' She said she would like to go out of the country and change her name. 'Joey would find you,' I told her. And she said, 'You're probably right.' "

Carla said Bobbie told her she was bleeding money away from Gymbags. "She said she'd record payments in the checkbook and (withdraw and) keep the money. ... She told me she'd bought a gun."

20.

Loretta Hendricks of Gastonia, Joey's sister, had once been the bookkeeper for Gymbags. She countered Bobbie's testimony that Joey had added Pro-Formance bumper stickers to Bobbie's Acura Legend on the morning of April 13, 1991.

"I drove that car for a couple of months around October 1990," Hendricks said. "We bought several Pro-Formance bumper stickers, and some were on the Acura Legend (then). To my knowledge, they were left there."

In cross-examination, Hendricks admitted that she didn't recall seeing the Acura during the period April 10-12, 1991.

21.

Elaine Neal, the Caldwells' next-door neighbor, testified that Barbara Caldwell "walked around the neighborhood" from about 10 a.m. to 11 a.m. on April 13, 1991, "asking if anyone had seen they (the Caldwells) were at home in their den watching TV (the night before). … She told me some friends of theirs had been murdered the night before, and she and Joey were suspects." Neal had told Bobbie that she and her husband had not observed the Caldwells' house at all the night before; they had been attending a Charlotte Hornets basketball game.

Neal also testified to the presence of a boyfriend in Bobbie's life: "One Saturday morning, I noticed the blinds in her house were turned differently than they had been. I called and asked if everything was all right. … I'm not sure (when this happened), May or June (of 1993). … She said she was not alone. She was with a gentleman named Kevin. I knew she was going with him, but I didn't know his last name. … I first saw Kevin three or four weeks after Joey's arrest. … I saw his vehicle parked at her house at night, sometimes in the morning, sometimes in the middle of the day."

The jury listened attentively to all the defense testimony, but it could not have escaped their notice that, with the exception of Elaine Neal — whose testimony was not particularly helpful to the defense — all the defense witnesses thus far had been relatives of Joey.

22.

Hewitt brought forward one more witness: Myron Mackey "Monte" Irvin of Charlotte, whose nickname derived from the name of an old-time major league baseball player. Irvin had been involved with the distribution of Pro-Formance.

He testified that Clyde Sullivan had tried various tactics to put a cash squeeze on Gymbags in order to gain the formula and trademark rights to the drink at a lower price.

"Clyde Sullivan called me in Oklahoma City," Irvin said on the stand, "and asked me to be involved with the distribution of Pro-Formance. I met with Joey Caldwell and Sullivan to set up a distribution network for Joey's sports drink. Sullivan was to establish a company as the marketing arm. I was to handle the East Coast. Drew Carver, from Phoenix, was to handle the West Coast and the military. We were trying to get Joey to sign a contract. We were getting $1 a case for every case that went through our network."

But, Irvin said, "We never got to the point of distribution."

"Why?" Hewitt asked.

"In my opinion," Irvin said, "Clyde Sullivan was a very unusual man to work with.

"We had a meeting of sixty Southeastern distributors — but we were instructed (by Sullivan) not to sign any of them up. ... the result was, we were not able to start distribution. ... Sullivan instructed us not to have any more contact with Joey Caldwell."

Later, Irvin said, "Everything was put on hold because Clyde and Joey had begun negotiations about selling (the rights to Pro-Formance)."

Still later, after those negotiations fell through, Irvin said, "I negotiated with Joey Caldwell on behalf of Maceo, myself, and Drew. We were to be equity owners in the company and to set up a distribution network."

(Maceo's company Ventures, Inc., eventually had several other stockholders as well, including his fellow Richmond County Commissioner Prentice Taylor and Richmond County banker and developer Claude Smith.)

23.

Joey's last chance at freedom was his own testimony. On the stand, he tried to explain his words on the SBI tape about "shells" in the McEachern house with a fantastic story of showing Maceo, during a visit to the McEacherns' home, a 9-millimeter handgun that Clyde Sullivan had just given Joey. He said Maceo pulled the ammunition clip out of the gun, and two cartridges came out and rolled underneath the sofa. Asked on cross-examination by Glaser why he had assured Bobbie on the tape that the "shells" would never be found, Joey said, "I would assume that Mrs. McEachern cleaned her house, and I assume she vacuumed them up or found them under the sofa and disposed of them."

He said he had not bought a gun in Garden City, Georgia, although he passed through the town on the way back from the visit to his mother in January

1991. He said he and Bobbie ate lunch at a Cracker Barrel restaurant there and that he stopped at a service station in Garden City and bought gasoline. "Bobbie used the car phone," he said, "while I was paying for the gas. She said she had called her mother, but that her mother wasn't home."

Joey explained his words on the tape about throwing his clothing into "the lakes" by saying that he had spilled Pro-Formance drink on his shirt and left the wet shirt in his car on a hot day. "It had soured. I drove to a bridge and tossed (the shirt) over the top of the car into the lake."

If those explanations sounded fantastic, so was Joey's attempt to describe what he had done and seen at Southpark Mall on the night of the murders. Bobbie had told him that the Charlotte Symphony had been performing in the mall's commons area, but on the stand Joey referred to the musical group as "a band."

"Was it a band or an orchestra?" Glaser asked on cross-examination.

"It was a bunch of people playing music, all right?" Joey retorted.

He said he could not remember any of the songs they had played. "It really wasn't my kind of music."

To questions by Hewitt, Joey told new stories about Clyde Sullivan's intimidating way of doing business and his temper. Once, he said, when he had called Sullivan from his car phone about some details of the distribution agreement, Sullivan became angry and told him, "Why don't you just stop your car on the side of the road, and I'll come up there and whip your ass right now." (That may have happened: It may have been the time that Joey left his briefcase at Sullivan's and called him, expressing anger of his own over Sullivan's allowing him to leave the house without his briefcase.)

Continuing his cross-examination, Glaser showed Joey several photographs of the McEacherns' mangled bodies, asking him repeatedly if he recognized them.

Joey appeared to show no emotion, although some courtroom observers interpreted his long silence as an attempt to fight back tears. "I never saw them like this," he finally said.

24.

Everyone in the courtroom but Joey, apparently, knew that his testimony was a flop. After the case went to the jury two days later, Joey telephoned from the High Point Jail to a friend, asking him to reserve a restaurant for a victory party that evening.

Joey's mother told a friend that the trial had so fascinated Joey that, "When this is all over, he's thinking about a career as a lawyer."

25.

Sandra Hairston made the initial closing argument for the prosecution — a brief statement in which she recapitulated Bobbie's testimony about Joey's activities on the night of April 12, 1991. She maintained that Joey did not leave home on April 10, 1991, until after dark — after he had received the telephone call from his father.

Hewitt's closing argument for the defense opened with the words, "Joey Caldwell does not stand before you charged with the crime of murder." He went on to argue that the prosecution's efforts to prove that Caldwell had murdered the McEacherns had been irrelevant to the weapons and money laundering charges.

"The conduct of mailing letters, spending money, buying Porsche automobiles, adding onto your house — none of that is illegal in itself," Hewitt said. "Spending two million dollars over the course of less than two years is not illegal — maybe it should be, but it isn't."

He reminded the jury that the descriptions of the man in the McEacherns' driveway by witnesses Margie Bohannon and Hughes Webster did not describe Joey Caldwell — who was five feet seven inches tall, not five feet ten, had short-cropped, straight black hair rather than bushy and sandy hair, and was said by his wife to have been wearing a hat and Army-fatigue camouflage clothing, not "casual clothes."

He made an attempt to inject Clyde Sullivan back into the case as a suspect, suggesting to the jury that the scenario of Sullivan's hiring someone to kill the McEacherns was a viable alternative to the prosecution's scenario. But Hewitt's heart wasn't in that argument: He mentioned it, perhaps to plant a seed of reasonable doubt in the minds of some jurors, then let it drop.

Hewitt pursued with considerably more vigor a scenario in which Bobbie made the whole story up. He reminded jurors that Bobbie had twice lied to grand juries, then had changed her story to the second grand jury, then during Joey's trial had revised part of what she had said earlier. "When do you believe her?" Hewitt said. "Which time, when she puts her hand on the Bible, do you believe her? This time, that time, that time, or that time — or any time? Or any time?" He suggested that she had three reasons to "turn in her husband and testify against him. She was trying to get out of her marriage. Money and greed. And the promise of immunity from prosecution."

What about Joey, he asked the jury. "What would motivate him to go down and kill Maceo McEachern and his mother? There was no rational motivation at all. Maceo was his star witness in a lawsuit."

Hewitt then turned to the ticklish issue of the SBI tape — the most damning piece of evidence in the trial. Earlier, he had won a concession from Judge

Osteen to disallow the jurors to consider the words in a transcript of the tape, which they were given in order to follow along while the tape was being played. The jurors were to consider only the words they heard on the tape itself, and many of those words were muffled or obscured by ambient sounds such as highway noise, the conversations of nearby diners in the restaurant, and the clatter of plates and utensils — even though the tape had been "enhanced" in the SBI Lab to remove as much of the ambient noise as possible.

"Recall the tape — what you could hear of it," Hewitt told the jury. "I would argue that you couldn't hear much of anything. I contend that the most important thing about that tape is that you can't make head nor tail of it."

Hewitt concluded his closing argument by saying that the McEacherns "were savagely killed by two blasts of a shotgun. And the only evidence you have that Joey Caldwell did that is Bobbie Caldwell."

26.

"You have a reasonable doubt?" Rick Glaser asked the jury in his closing argument. "Look at this. He (Hewitt) didn't address that. Because he (pointing at Joey) did it." Glaser walked over to the defense table, stared down at Joey, and pointed at him. "He's the killer."

"Please don't address the defendant," Osteen warned.

"Sorry, your honor," Glaser said, and strode back to the jury box. But several times during his address, he returned to look down at Caldwell.

Glaser turned to the question of Bobbie Caldwell's veracity, reminding the jurors that other evidence had corroborated most of what she had said in her testimony. "Is she a psychic?" Glaser asked rhetorically. "Can she just grab things out of the air and come up with things that are completely corroborated? Is she psychic? No. She was with him in this whole thing to kill these people. ... She got scared because the money was running short — and you know what else? She's the one witness this man has confided in. They're a team — a lethal, diabolical team. ... How'd she know the house had a hearth in it?"

He walked the jury through Bobbie's testimony about the shotgun and the concrete block, and the corroborating testimony by SBI forensics experts and by Chris Cox, whom Vela had told about the concrete block. "Listen," Glaser said, pausing dramatically. "From the grave, she's telling you who killed her." He turned back to Joey. "It's his plan — his doing — his murder."

(In the spectators' area of the courtroom, Carla Peoples turned to her husband and whispered, "When this is over, we're going to sue him for defaming Joey's character.")

Glaser addressed what Hewitt had said about the descriptions of the murderer by the McEacherns' driveway. "This is a man who can alter his appearance. Different hair style, different complexion, different weight — it just depends on the clothing." Mrs. Bohannon might have said the man was five-ten, Glaser admitted, "but she also told you he wasn't as tall as she was, and she's five-eight."

Glaser asked the jury whether they had noticed that, "When he (Joey) lied, he blinked. But he didn't blink at least one time, when he looked at the destruction he had wrought — when he looked at (photographs of) the people he killed."

Glaser read the jurors many excerpts from the tape transcript, over Hewitt's objections. "Why would he (Joey) be concerned about showing Maceo McEachern a gun in October 1990?" he asked.

He returned to the question of Bobbie's veracity. "Why would Barbara Caldwell frame him and then, of all things, come up with a story that she's involved? Why frame herself? She's been promised nothing; she expects to be prosecuted."

Glaser wound up his argument by staring at Joey again and addressing the contention that Joey would not have killed the McEacherns because he needed Maceo to testify in the lawsuit against Sullivan.

"A lawsuit would be long and expensive," Glaser said. "Why do you need him for a lawsuit, when you can kill him for two million dollars?"

27.

Eleven of the jurors were convinced almost from the outset of deliberations that Joey was guilty. But one female juror held out, saying that she believed that Bobbie had made the whole story up in order to rid herself of her husband.

After several hours of deliberations, the jurors sent word to Osteen that they had reached a verdict on one count (that verdict turned out to be "not guilty" of witness tampering) but were deadlocked on the other 57.

"It has to be not guilty of witness tampering," Hewitt said during a break in the courthouse canteen. "That's the only charge that doesn't depend on any of the other charges."

"Maybe it's 'guilty' of witness tampering, and they'll find him 'not guilty' of the other 58," a kibitzer said.

"I'd take that and run with it," Hewitt replied.

The jury's quick decision on the jury-tampering charge had to buoy Hewitt's spirits, however. Bobbie had said on the witness stand that, after the federal grand jury subpoenaed her in January 1993 for a second round of testimony — at Glaser's urging, after he read the proffer from attorney Eben Rawls about "Client X" —

she and Joey had a conversation "concerning keeping the same story that we had had before." She added, "He wanted me to be consistent with the statements that I had made (to) the previous grand jury." In other words, he had coached her to lie to the grand jury again. Bobbie's testimony on the point was clear, concise and consistent with the rest of her testimony. If the jurors believed her, surely they would have found Joey guilty of tampering with a witness.

That they had presumably found him not guilty was a good sign for the defense. It meant that they did not trust Bobbie's testimony — and the whole case depended on Bobbie's testimony.

28.

After nine hours of deliberations, the jurors announced that they were still deadlocked — more good news, it appeared, for the defense. Osteen ordered them back into the courtroom, and the jury foreman asked him whether the jurors were only to consider Osteen's instructions to the jury, or whether they could also consider the language of the indictment. Osteen told them that they could consider the indictment also, as well as any other evidence that had been presented, and that they should concentrate on resolving their differences and make every effort to arrive at a unanimous opinion.

Jury deliberation went into a second day. Later some jurors revealed that one female juror was the lone holdout. She was adamant in her conviction that Bobbie had made the whole story up in order to "get rid of" Joey, so that she could make a new life for herself.

Other jurors pleaded with her to consider the other testimony and the few items of physical evidence in concert with Bobbie's testimony. They pointed to the telephone bills, the wadding from the shotgun shells, the gun-shop application form, and the testimony by Randy Riggins that Joey and Barbara were eager to get Maceo's key man insurance policies in force and that Bobbie had picked up their copy of the second insurance policy on April 10, just two days before the murders.

The holdout juror was unconvinced.

Then the conversation in the jury room turned to a couple of key pieces of physical evidence that only the police and the murderer had known about — the broken frying pan in Vela's house, and the concrete block in her front yard. Bobbie had mentioned both in her testimony, and she could not have known about them if she had not been a confederate of the murderer.

The holdout juror came around. The frying pan and the concrete block were tangible items of evidence that could not be refuted by any estimate of Bobbie's character or truthfulness.

(Actually, the police had not totally succeeded in keeping the two pieces of evidence secret. Many people had been at the scene on April 12, 1991, and word got out in Richmond County about the broken frying pan. Besides, Chris Cox had told a number of people about his conversation with Vela concerning the concrete block, and they had told others. There was, however, no way that Bobbie could have learned about the frying pan and the block except through Joey.)

29.

On September 1, 1993, bailiffs called Joey into the courtroom to hear the verdict. Despite warnings by his attorneys that the verdict may go against him, Joey still exuded confidence and optimism. As he entered the courtroom, escorted by federal marshals at each elbow, he wore the same gray suit he had worn on the second day of the trial — the long day of Bobbie's testimony. He grinned at Bobby Peoples, Jr., who was sitting in the first row of spectators, and gave the "thumbs up" sign.

Joey was found not guilty of witness tampering, but the jury found him guilty of 57 counts of weapons violations, mail fraud, and money laundering. He figured to be sentenced to a minimum of 40 years in prison, without possibility of parole. He showed no emotion when the verdicts were read. While, at Hewitt's request, a bailiff polled the jury, asking them each to state that they had voted "guilty," Joyce Southard and Carla Peoples cried silently.

Floy Dean Caldwell sat slumped in his chair, looking at the floor. He had arrived for the first day of the trial looking confident — but, driving up to Greensboro from Gastonia each day and slowly being confronted with the weight of the evidence, he had taken on a morose expression. Courtroom observers felt that he had believed his son innocent — until he heard the testimony.

30.

One of the federal marshals who served as bailiffs during the trial had been a homicide detective for most of his earlier 20-year career in the Richmond, Virginia, Police Department.

"Of all the hundreds of murder trials I've seen," he said," this one had the greatest weight of evidence on the prosecution side. I was amazed that the jury deliberated so long. I can't imagine anybody's hearing that testimony and having any shred of doubt as to Caldwell's guilt."

Terry Moore was jubilant at the verdict.

"I think this has been the best example you could ever see of law enforcement agencies and the court system working in concert to catch and convict a criminal," he said. "Just think about all the time and all the man-hours from different agencies that went into this effort: the Hamlet Police Department, the Richmond County Sheriff's Department, the SBI, the federal prosecutor's office. This case has been a once-in-a-lifetime thing, and I'm proud of every law officer and every U.S. attorney who had a part in it."

X.

AFTERMATH

1.

Late that night, Joey Caldwell committed suicide by hanging himself from a bed sheet in the High Point Jail.

He had gone to some pains to make his suicide successful —stuffing toilet paper into his mouth to keep himself from crying out; wrapping his mouth and nose with socks to cut off his breath once he lost consciousness; and tying his hands together with socks, then drawing them over his feet and behind his back. He tied the sheet to a vent that extended from the wall; the vent was not high enough for him to suspend himself from it without touching the floor, and so he had to draw his legs up underneath him.

This suicide was no "cry for help." It was the suicide of a man absolutely determined to die.

He left a brief note to his jailers, a longer one to relatives, and a lengthy one to his wife.

The note to Bobbie Caldwell began, "At last the lying is over."

Joey Caldwell died on the 86th anniversary of Vela McEachern's birth. "Vela got her birthday present last night," funeral home employee Chris Cox crowed when he heard the news.

2.

No one was more surprised at Joey's suicide than Larry Hewitt. He had visited Joey in the lockup a few hours after the jury returned its verdict, to reassure him that the case was not yet over. Hewitt planned to appeal the verdict on the grounds that the SBI's planting a recording device on Bobbie on March 11, 1993, constituted illegal entrapment and that the tape should never have been allowed as evidence.

Hewitt's associate Richard Fennell had argued in court that the tape should

Last Photo Of Caldwell

Joey Caldwell is pictured in handcuffs outside the Middle District Federal Courthouse in Greensboro last Monday, just prior to being escorted into court by U.S. marshals — one of whom is partially visible at left. Caldwell committed suicide in his High Point Jail cell Thursday morning, just hours after he was convicted of 57 charges of fraud, weapons violations, conspiracy, and money laundering linked to a plot to kill Macon McEachern of Hamlet for insurance money. Prosecutors said Caldwell was the triggerman in the April 12, 1991, slayings of McEachern, 43, and his mother Vela McEachern, 83. (AP photo)

Associated Press picture of Joey Caldwell in handcuffs in the last week of his life, in the Richmond County Daily Journal, September 1993. Photo by Clark Cox. Clipping from the collection of Naomi Daggs.

not be allowed as evidence of a conspiracy because any alleged conspiracy to murder Maceo and cover up the crime would have ended when Bobbie "became, in effect, a government agent," cooperating with the lawmen to trap her husband. Osteen had not agreed, saying, "I am reasonably convinced that once a husband and wife begin to talk about criminal activity, and participate in plans for criminal activity, that any conversations thereafter about it, whether the criminal activity is still going on or not going on, is not a violation of the privilege (of confidential communication between spouses)."

But Hewitt told Joey that he thought there was a good chance that the federal appeals court panel would agree with the entrapment argument and order a new trial, *sans* tape. And without the tape, after all, the case boiled down to Joey's word against Bobbie's, with some evidence available that Bobbie was planning to "get rid of" Joey so that she could make a new life.

Evidently, despite Hewitt's reassurances, Joey had decided that he didn't have the stomach to keep lying.

3.

Judge Osteen convened the Caldwell trial's jurors the morning after Joey's suicide. "You should not blame yourself in any way for what happened last night," he told them.

"You made the right decision."

4.

Terry Moore said he took no pleasure in Caldwell's suicide.

"This whole case was an example of greed and values in the wrong places," he said. "Not just a few people got hurt. I feel terrible for Joey Caldwell's family."

5.

Smith Middle School in Charlotte, where Bobbie was a teacher, placed her on leave shortly after her testimony in her husband's trial became public knowledge.

She continued to operate the Nutrin Labs business from her home.

Within a few weeks after Joey's arrest, Bobbie had reestablished a relationship with a former boyfriend, Kevin Kessell. But by the time of Joey's trial, she testified under questioning by Larry Hewitt, she had stopped dating Kessell.

In January 1994, she pleaded guilty to conspiring to launder money and to lying to a federal grand jury. The maximum sentence for those crimes is 10 years in federal prison. But because she had cooperated with prosecutors in the trial of her husband, the prosecutors in her case urged a more lenient sentence of 18 to 25 months — the minimum permitted.

On March 31, 1994, Judge Osteen sentenced her to five years in federal prison. Under federal sentencing guidelines, she would be required to serve four and one-half years of the sentence — after which, she would be required to submit to three years of supervised release, with 100 hours of "community service" work each year.

Bobbie reported for custody on May 2, 1994. She served the sentence in women's federal prisons in Lexington, Kentucky, and Butner, North Carolina. She was released in late 1998.

At the sentencing hearing in 1994, Bobbie presented an image of a repentant woman, sitting quietly through the three hours of testimony, wearing a long navy sweater and skirt. She spoke only three words during the hearing. When Osteen asked if she had anything to say in her defense before he pronounced sentence, she said, "No, your honor."

Outside the courtroom in Greensboro after her sentencing, Bobbie had more to say. She sought out Naomi Daggs and told her, according to one eyewitness: "I have this deep sorrow I feel that won't go away. I think about you every day. I know what you lost. ... I deserve to feel this pain and this suffering."

Naomi, whose blue and white polka-dot dress had, coincidentally, the same shade of blue as Bobbie's outfit, responded: "I bear you no ill will. ... I pity you."

6.

Earlier that day, however, Naomi had delivered an impassioned plea to Osteen to impose "the maximum sentence allowed by law" on Bobbie. She spoke movingly and at length of the anguish and sense of loss the Richmond County community suffered over the deaths of the McEacherns.

"I think (my testimony) made a difference," she said after the sentencing.

Her testimony is worth quoting in full, to illustrate the pain and suffering undergone by those whose loved ones die untimely deaths by violence:

Your honor, I am Naomi Daggs. I teach English at Richmond Community College in Hamlet, North Carolina. For eighteen and one-half years, I was involved either platonically or romantically with Maceo McEachern. For most of those years, I was the main woman in his life. I became closer to him than anyone. He was not a perfect man, and ours was not a perfect relationship, but anyone who knew both of us would tell you how deeply we loved each other. In fact, his last words to me, just an hour or two from his dying moment, were, "Ma Ma, you know I love you." For the last twelve years of his life, I spent time with him almost every day, and talked to him by phone on the few days we didn't see each other. I knew his dreams, his faults, his strengths, his virtues, his secrets.

Better than anyone, I know what a loss his death has been.

I am here to implore the court to give Mrs. Caldwell the maximum sentence allowed by law. Your honor, you have explored the mechanics of this crime, this heinous crime. You have heard a clinical analysis of the events and the diabolical thought processes that led to the death of Maceo and his mother. I am sure you have undoubtedly weighed her cooperation with the District Attorney's office in your deliberations. And we just heard Mrs. Caldwell's attorney and two witnesses talk about the pathology of her relationship with her domineering, sociopathic husband, which causes me to wonder: If she was so completely under Joey's domination, should I assume that if he told her to, she would have willingly pulled the shotgun trigger and blown Maceo's face off? So I hope you also will look again at the gruesome photographs showing how Joey Caldwell's shotgun blast destroyed Maceo's face and maimed his body as his mother watched help-lessly, hopelessly, in horror. And I hope you consider that the photographs and evidence, however, still don't show the terrible human price paid in the last few moments of the life of this still vibrant, still productive 83-year-old mother as she watched her beloved only child, her heart of hearts, die in such an untimely, ignoble way, and then to meet the same fate herself in a few moments.

Anyone at the (Joey's) trial or reading one of the numerous articles written about it must have cringed in horror at the cost Maceo and his mother paid so that Mrs. Caldwell and her husband could pay some of their bills, redecorate their home, drive better cars, and squander their blood money on status symbols and plastic surgery. Surely, real justice demands more than a reduced sentence for anyone responsible, even in the planning and cover-up stages, for such an unspeakable act.

And in your consideration of the gravity of Mrs. Caldwell's crime, please look at the other cost, the one little has been said about — the human loss: the emotional robbery that Bobbie and Joey Caldwell have perpetrated on others, including their own families.

I ask the court today to look at this loss through the eyes of the Caldwells' other victims.

Look through the eyes of Maceo and Vela's family — robbed of a loving man who brought pride and happiness to them, and robbed of a loving aunt and sister who served as a beacon of strength and joy.

When you weigh the appropriate punishment for this woman, look through the eyes of Maceo's friends — robbed of his laughter, his fellowship, his companionship.

Look through the eyes of a community still suffering quietly from the loss of two people genuinely important to so many — Maceo and his mother weren't just "those people," faceless people in their community — they were not just important in status, but important as extended family to many. They were one-of-a-kind people who helped give a community its 'personality,' its human face.

I ask you to look through the eyes of Sara Hamilton, a retired school administrator who recently asked if we could plan some kind of community memorial service. Her reason? She believes that others are like her — she was not a close personal friend of Maceo's, but her sense of loss over the waste, the void in the community, the injustice, simply will not subside; she desperately needs closure. She wonders if a service will help to heal this gaping, still festering community wound.

Naomi told about Maceo's help to Mildred Stanback, saying, "I can certainly tell the price Mildred is paying to help the Caldwells live in luxury, when to this very day, whenever I see her, tears form in her eyes at the mention of Vela or Maceo."

And she told of his charity toward his "little old man" in Hamlet, saying, "I cannot imagine the cost (of Maceo's death) to (the man). ... And I don't even know what has since happened to him, but I can imagine how empty his world must be now."

She continued:

I want you to know about Maceo's good friend, Sydney Hodges, a burly, gruff bodybuilder and pawnshop owner, whose pain shows in his eyes when he tells me that not a single day goes by that he doesn't think of his buddy and how much he misses him.

I hope, your honor, that in making your decision, you can look through the eyes and heart of Dr. Wendell Wells, Maceo's closest friend — for months so grief-stricken that his blood pressure wouldn't go down and his wife feared he'd have a stroke or nervous breakdown.

Or Michael McInnis, Maceo's close friend and partner in 4M Quarter Horses, who quietly internalizes his loss, but who, like me, has not been back to a restaurant we used to frequent — because it was Maceo's favorite restaurant — since April 1991. That's three, that's three whole years.

And nothing more dramatically shows the insidious way the Caldwells' crime has disrupted the lives of our community than the former funeral home employee, Clyde Harrington, the elderly gentleman who testified at the trial about what he saw through the window when he was sent to see what was going on at Mrs. McEachern's that horrible night. What was not evident from Mr. Harrington's testimony was that he was not in good health at the time of the murders, and the trauma of the murders nearly killed him. He had to go back into the hospital. When I rode back to Rockingham with him after his testimony, this is how he described his ordeal: 'I thought that thing was going to take me away from here.'

So you see, your honor, the people who loved and cared about Maceo and his mom have been robbed of an important part of their lives, robbed in such a brutal way that the McEacherns' mortal wounds have become scars on their own hearts.

Wounds that will not heal.

These and dozens like them are the Caldwells' other victims. From people who knew Maceo well to those who didn't but still say, with real sincerity, when they run into me out in the community, 'You know, it's just not the same around here with him gone.'

Indeed, the quality of mercy will not be strained if you dispense the full sentence for Mrs. Caldwell's part in this unspeakable crime.

I have not spoken much of my own loss, but if any of you think I have escaped this pain, you are mistaken. My anguish goes so deep. I still can't describe it well. Let me just say that, like my little community but a thousand times a thousand more, my heart is deeply wounded.

*The great American author, Nathaniel Hawthorne, believed that the
greatest sin is violating the sanctity of the human heart. I believe that. I
think it should also be a crime.*

7.

Rockingham attorney Richard G. "Ric" Buckner, acting on behalf of the
McEachern heirs — Vela's brother and sister and a nephew, all of whom lived in
the Winston-Salem, North Carolina, area, sued Sun Life Assurance Company and
Great West Life Assurance Company, claiming that the insurance companies' un-
derwriting departments had been negligent in issuing the policies without informing
Maceo of their full face value and without studying whether the income projections
justified that amount of insurance on an initial $235,000 debt, $40,000 of which had
already been paid. It was Buckner's contention that the insurance companies un-
wittingly assisted the Caldwells in creating the motive for murdering the
McEacherns, by making Maceo more valuable to them dead than alive.

On April 6, 1995, Sun Life entered into a consent agreement with the
heirs, agreeing to pay a total of $175,000 in settlement of their claim.

Shortly thereafter, a U.S. District Court judge dismissed the suit against
Great West, saying that the plaintiffs could not sustain a suit against an insurance carrier on the facts presented.

"We were fortunate," Buckner said, "in being able to settle the Sun Life
suit before the Great West dismissal created a precedent."

8.

On March 28, 1996, a civil court judge in Guilford County ordered Bobbie
Caldwell and two minority shareholders in the Caldwells' company Gymbags to
pay $31.5 million to the heirs of Maceo and Vela McEachern — Vela's brother
and sister and a nephew, all of whom lived in the Winston-Salem, North Carolina, area. It was one of the largest wrongful-death monetary awards in the history of North Carolina up to that time — possibly the largest ever.

Buckner, who also represented the McEachern heirs in this case, said
he doubted that any of the money would ever be collected, since the federal
government had seized the Caldwells' assets for payment of claims arising
out of Joey Caldwell's money-laundering conviction. He said the court would
have claims, however, against assets that "may accrue in the future" to Bobbie
Caldwell.

Later that year, the McEachern heirs won a $1,133,930 judgment against
several other minority shareholders in Gymbags. Buckner said that the heirs

received "significant" payments as a result of the lawsuits, although the payments were far short of the amounts ordered to be paid.

"The important thing, to the heirs," Buckner said, "is that for the first time, a court in North Carolina has adjudged that Joey Caldwell murdered Vela and Maceo McEachern. The heirs wanted that on the record."

9.

What became of Bobbie Caldwell after her three years of supervised prison release came to an end in 2001? I was unable to reach her for this book, but there are some intriguing theories.

Considering the debts handing over he head – millions of dollars to the IRS, the insurance companies, the McEachern heirs – she will likely never be free of financial concerns.

But Carla Peoples testified during Joey's trial that Bobbie had told her that she had cash hidden away – a total of $160,000 that Joey, perhaps, didn't know of about. And during cross- examination in Joey's trial, she admitted to Larry Hewitt that, between them, she and Joey had withdrawn a total of about $318,000 in cash from two checking accounts and one money market savings account between October 1991 and April 1993. She said that, even though some of the cash withdrawals were in excess of $20,000, she could not recall how any of the money had been spent.

She could be far away, living on the money she had stashed away.

Or she may be working again, somewhere, as a teacher.

No one could tell me where she is.

10.

On June 15, 1996, Barbara M. Sullivan suffered a heart attack at the Sullivans' home near Southern Pines.

Shortly after she was taken away from the couple's Six Pillars Horse Farm by ambulance, Clyde Sullivan shot himself. He died the next day. Barbara Sullivan died in FirstHealth Moore Regional Hospital 10 days later.

Rumors claimed that Barbara Sullivan had been beaten (or poisoned) prior to her heart attack. The official autopsy report debunked the rumors. Dr. H.G. Marrow, who performed the autopsy, said, "There was no indication of a beating, homicide, suicide, or any evidence of poisoning or an overdose. She had some heart pathology that is consistent with the cause of death. It was basically a heart attack."

Perhaps the greatest mystery in the whole tragic story is that of why Clyde Sullivan decided to end his own life. Did some trauma, the nature of which may never be known, cause both Barbara Sullivan's heart attack and Clyde Sullivan's decision to commit suicide?

11.

Nathan and Carolyn Arthur, of Arcadia Farms, wound up with the formula and marketing rights to Pro-Formance.

But the rest of the original marketing team — those who were still alive — moved on to other pursuits. Monte Irvin, for example, became successful as a marketer of a popular line of fruit-based soft drinks, similar in composition to Pro-Formance, with the brand name Mistic.

Pro-Formance stayed around for a while in gyms and workout centers, but it never reestablished the retail presence it had possessed during Maceo's brief time as its trademark owner.

It was as if the drink had been cursed.

12.

Three businessmen joined forces in 1990 to distribute a sports drink. Soon after, they became combatants in disputes over money.

None of the three could possibly have foreseen, when their economic futures seemed so bright in 1990, that within six years they would all have suffered death by violence — one at the hands of another, and the other two by their own hands.

No one will ever know how much the Richmond County community lost in the deaths of Maceo and Vela McEachern.

No one will ever know why Clyde Sullivan committed suicide.

And no one will ever know for certain what made Joey Caldwell into a callous, conniving criminal.

But there is no scarcity of theories.

13.

Maceo's burning desire for a life of wealth and independence sowed the seeds of his undoing.

By most reasonable standards, Maceo was well off financially. Though he worked for his mother at the funeral home, he no longer lived with her and was no longer dependent on her for his livelihood. He had a number of other thriving business interests quite apart from Pro-Formance. He drove a late-model Lincoln, traveled widely, and was one of the most respected men in his community.

But Maceo had a vision of a better life. He wanted wealth, and he wanted the absolute independence that wealth could bring.

"The main thing," Naomi said, "was that he wanted to be free of his mother. That's why he went to such lengths to get economic freedom. He didn't know that, in order to be free of her, all he had to do was to give himself permission to be free."

Had Maceo not sought wealth, he would never have become involved with Joey Caldwell and Clyde Sullivan, two men whose sharp business dealings were foreign to his experience and whose penchant for violence were foreign to his nature.

14.

Some lawmen point to Bobbie Caldwell as the instigator of Joey Caldwell's crimes. Joey was so obsessed with his good-looking wife that he wanted to be with her all the time. He was demanding of her, urging her to have the breast implants and the liposuction that made her look even more attractive in his eyes. He controlled her even to the point of telling her what clothing to buy and choosing the outfit she would wear each day. But some have suggested that she exerted subtle pressures on him to provide the couple with money to indulge the lavish lifestyle she craved.

If Bobbie's testimony that she was fearful of Joey can be trusted, however, it gives the lie to the theory of Bobbie as instigator. And the testimony was corroborated by a neighbor and a relative, both of whom told of how she gave voice to her fears well before 1992.

"I don't think there's any doubt," said Terry Moore, "that if the Caldwells had stayed together, one of them would have eventually killed the other. And what I really believe is that if she hadn't turned him in, he would have killed her. Joey Caldwell did some horrible, terrible things in his life, and he wouldn't have balked at murdering his wife — whether for her life insurance, or just because he knew she was the only one who knew enough about the murders to pin them on him."

Moore finds the origin of Joey's crimes in his upbringing in a broken home, and the fact that his parents indulged him in bizarre behavior early on, encouraging him to become self-absorbed and self-indulgent to the point of disregarding others' feelings. He was obsessed with image, and keeping up the image he wanted to project to the world took more money than he was ever able to earn by legitimate means.

Whoever was the prime mover in the McEachern murders — whether

Joey or Bobbie, or whether they acted in concert from the beginning — the motivation boiled down to simple greed.

I think the prime mover was Joey, although I agree with Naomi Daggs that Bobbie may well have worked out the actual details of the murder plot. And I think his greed had deep psychological roots.

Amateur psychology is full of pitfalls, but there seems more than enough evidence to classify Joey as a narcissistic personality. Such personalities are obsessed with their own images and with their need to control everything in their own lives and in the lives of everyone around them. Their obsessions are so overriding that the true narcissist tends to discount the needs and feelings of others — as Joey did with the McEacherns and, indeed, with his own wife, Bobbie, whom he attempted to control every minute of the day. Her image as a "trophy wife" became important to him as part of his own image, and his "gift" of liposuction and breast enhancement was probably more a gift to himself than to her.

Psychologists are divided over whether narcissism is genetic in origin or has its origin in early life. Possibly both play a part. One theory has it that a person forms a narcissistic personality — with its inflated self-image and its inflated ideas of self-importance — in reaction to memories of a childhood in which one was deprived, demeaned, taunted, or derided. Those narcissists who turn to violence in later life, in order to maintain control over others, have often been the victims of violence in childhood.

There is no evidence that Joey was treated violently as a child, although discipline may well have been harsh in the Caldwell household: Floy Dean Caldwell was, after all, a military man, and military households are often run with strict regard for the "commander's" dictates and with punishments being meted out for the slightest infractions. More likely, though, Joey's childhood trauma came from being the product of a home in which quarreling and dissension were the norm. He may have chosen to stay in his room and not accompany his family on outings in order to distance himself from that dissension. It was during the period when he took his meals in his room that the obsession with self-image began to manifest itself, in his insistence on keeping his food and clothing separate from the food and clothing of other family members, doing his own laundry, and folding his own clothes just right.

Later, a taunt from a female classmate seems to have stiffened Joey's resolve to "make something of himself," and he moved out of his mother's home and began to concentrate on his body image, working out daily and transforming himself from a slight teen-ager into a state karate champion.

The continued obsession with self-image forced Joey to lead an ever more expensive lifestyle, with thousand-dollar suits and a big house, Mercedes and Porsche automobiles, a boat, and a succession of business ventures that always failed. Finally, he could not support the lifestyle without figuring out some way to make millions of dollars in a hurry.

That's when he and Bobbie hatched the murder scheme. It was bound to fail, for here was a man who failed in almost everything he attempted — dropping out of high school, divorcing three times, building an image that others would have found laughable had not his crimes been so horrible.

Joey's crimes, whatever their origin, were an offense against humanity. He ultimately decided to kill himself rather than pay the price society exacts for such crimes. In the end, gasping out his last breaths in a jail cell, he had as little respect for his own life as he showed for the lives of Maceo and Vela McEachern when he shotgunned them to death in their home. His apologies in his suicide notes did nothing to undo the damage he had done.

Psychology is one thing; morality is another. Morally, it is difficult to understand what turned the Joey Caldwell his family loved, the Joey Caldwell who at some point in his twisted life had a great potential for good, into the inhuman monster he became.

Joey was wont to blame others for his failures: his wives, his business partners, his (real or imagined) enemies — even the lawmen who pursued him and the prosecuting attorneys who found the flaws in his flimsy alibis.

But in the end, it was not the criminal justice system that brought Joey down. It was not his wife, not his business associates, not anyone else to whom he might have pointed.

It was Joey Caldwell himself.

SOURCES FOR
Deadly Greed

Personal Interviews
    Glenn Sumpter, 1991, 1992, 1993, 1994, 2000
    Terry Moore, 1991, 1992, 1993, 1994, 2000
    Naomi Daggs, 1991, 2000, 2002
    Chris Cox, 1991, 1992, 1993
    Helen Cox, 1991, 1994
    Catherine Monk, 1993
    Pat Byrd, 1994
    Wilson Moore, 1994
    Don McCluskey, 1996
    Ric Buckner, 1996
    Robert Bristow, 2002
    Dale Furr, 2002

Audiotape
    State Bureau of Investigation tape of conversation between Joey Caldwell and Bobbi[e] Caldwell, March 11, 1993

Videotape
    State Bureau of Investigation video of Joey & Bobbi[e] Caldwell's home, 1993

Court Records
    Transcript: *United States of America v. Joey Dean Caldwell*, August 20-September 1, 1993. United States District Court for the Middle District of North Carolina, Greensboro.

    Complaint: *Jacqueline Raines Dunlap, administratrix of the estate of Maceo Raines McEachern, and Jacqueline Raines Dunlap, administratrix of the estate of Vela Raines McEachern, v. Barbara Burford Caldwell, Steve Smith, Clyde Sullivan, Lee Sullivan, Vince Harrelson, Jeff Bridges, Randy Riggins, and Louis Bridges*, August 1, 1994. Richmond County, N.C., Superior Court, Rockingham.

    Mediation Memorandum: *Jacqueline Raines Dunlap, administratrix of the estate of Maceo Raines McEachern, and Jacqueline Raines Dunlap, administratrix of the estate of Vela Raines McEachern, v. Sun Life Assurance Co. of Canada,* July 18, 1994. U.S. District Court for the Middle District of North Carolina, Greensboro.

Consent Order: *Jacqueline Raines Dunlap, administratrix of the estate of Maceo Raines McEachern, and Jacqueline Raines Dunlap, administratrix of the estate of Vela Raines McEachern, v. Sun Life Assurance Co. of Canada,* April 16, 1995. Richmond County, N.C., Superior Court, Rockingham.

Judgment and Order: *Jacqueline Raines Dunlap, administratrix of the estate of Maceo Raines McEachern, and Jacqueline Raines Dunlap, administratrix of the estate of Vela Raines McEachern, v. John R. Daniel, administrator of the estate of Joey Dean Caldwell, Barbara Burford Caldwell, and Gymbags Inc. March 1996.* Richmond County, N.C., Superior Court, Rockingham.

Petition for Rehearing: *Jacqueline Raines Dunlap, administratrix of the estate of Maceo Raines McEachern, and Jacqueline Raines Dunlap, administratrix of the estate of Vela Raines McEachern, v. The Great-West Life Assurance Co.,* April 16, 1996. United States Court of Appeals for the Fourth Circuit, Richmond, Va.

Judgment and Order: *Jacqueline Raines Dunlap, administratrix of the estate of Maceo Raines McEachern, and Jacqueline Raines Dunlap, administratrix of the estate of Vela Raines McEachern, v. Barbara Burford Caldwell, Nationsbank, executor of the estate of Clyde Sullivan, Nationsbank, executor of the estate of Barbara Sullivan, Vince Harrelson, Jeff Bridges, Randy Riggins, and Louis Bridges,* October 23, 1996. Richmond County, N.C., Superior Court, Rockingham.

Newspaper Articles

"County Shocked by 'Execution-Style' Deaths of McEacherns," by Glenn Sumpter. *The Richmond County Daily Journal,* April 14, 1991.

"Police Seeking a Car with Canadian Plates," by Jeff Holland. *The Richmond County Daily Journal,* April 15, 1991.

"The Talk of The County: Hamlet Slayings Remain a Mystery," by Paige Williams. *The Charlotte Observer,* April 15, 1991.

"Mecklenburg County Lawsuit Related to Maceo McEachern Drawing Interest of Police," by Jeff Holland. *The Richmond County Daily Journal,* April 16, 1991.

"Victim Was Set To Testify; $2 Million Suit Alleges Conspiracy," by Joseph Menn and Paige Williams. *The Charlotte Observer,* April 16, 1991.

"Governor Offers $10,000 Reward," *The Richmond County Daily Journal,* April 17, 1991.

"McEachern Suspect Is Unidentified," *The Richmond County Daily Journal,* April 18, 1991.

"Overflow Crowd Attends Funeral," by Glenn Sumpter. *The Richmond County Daily Journal,* April 19, 1991.

"No New Leads in McEachern Murder Case," by Jeff Holland. *The Richmond County Daily Journal,* May 1, 1991

"Life Insurance Claim, Lawsuits over Sports-Drink Firm Settled," by Joseph Menn. *The Charlotte Observer,* September 20, 1991.

"Unsolved Murders Haunt SBI Team: About Half of Cases Assigned to Special Unit Elude Answers," by Sue Price Wilson. *The Charlotte Observer(fourth edition),* January 4, 1993.

"Arrest Made in McEachern Murder Case," *The Richmond County Daily Journal*, March 12, 1993.

"Wife's Affidavit Led to Arrest in McEachern Case," *The Richmond County Daily Journal*, March 14, 1993.

"Joey Caldwell Denied Bond," *The Richmond County Daily Journal*, March 16, 1993.

"Caldwell Bound Over for Action by Grand Jury," by Clark Cox. *The Richmond County Daily Journal*, March 28, 1993.

"Caldwell Indicted for Hamlet Murders," *The Richmond County Daily Journal*, March 30, 1993.

"Caldwell Trial Underway in Federal Court," *The Richmond County Daily Journal*, August 24, 1993.

"Prosecutor Outlines Alibi Plans in Case against Caldwell," by Joseph Menn. *The Charlotte Observer*, August 24, 1993.

"McEachern Was Not Original Murder Target," *The Richmond County Daily Journal*, August 25, 1993.

"Caldwell's Wife Tells Court How They Plotted to Kill McEachern," by Joseph Menn. *The Charlotte Observer*, Aug. 25, 1993."Jurors in Caldwell Trial Hear 'Smoking Gun' Tape," by Clark Cox. *The Richmond County Daily Journal*, August 26, 1993.

"Money from McEachern's Life Insurance Policies Is Gone," by Clark Cox. *The Richmond County Daily Journal*, August 26, 1993.

"Prosecution Rests in Caldwell Trial," by Clark Cox. *The Richmond County Daily Journal*, August 27, 1993.

"Closing Arguments Begin Monday," by Clark Cox. *The Richmond County Daily Journal*, August 28, 1993.

"Caldwell Jury Is Expected To Get Case Late This Afternoon," by Clark Cox. *The Richmond County Daily Journal*, August 30, 1993.

"Fate of Caldwell in Hands of Jury," by Clark Cox. *The Richmond County Daily Journal*, August 31, 1993.

"Jury Is Deadlocked on 57 of 58 Charges," by Clark Cox. *The Richmond County Daily Journal*, September 1, 1993.

"Joey Caldwell Commits Suicide," by Clark Cox. *The Richmond County*

Daily Journal, September 2, 1993.

"Jury Found Caldwell Guilty on 57 of 58 Counts," by Clark Cox. *The Richmond County Daily Journal*, September 2, 1993.

"Caldwell's Note's Content Is Secret," *The Richmond County Daily Journal*, September 3, 1993.

"Assessing the Caldwell Case (editorial)," *The Richmond County Daily Journal*, September 5, 1993.

"Dreams of Riches, Acts of Betrayal," by Joseph Menn. *The Charlotte Observer*, November 28, 1993.

"Alibis Stop Investigators like a Concrete Block," by Joseph Menn. *The Charlotte Observer*, November 29, 1993.

"Client X Gives Investigators Break Needed To Solve Case," by Joseph Menn. *The Charlotte* Observer, November 30, 1993.

"Criminals in the Classroom: N.C. Is Slow To Revoke Teaching Credentials." *The Charlotte Observer*, March 22, 1994.

"Barbara Caldwell Sentenced to 5 Years," by John Hechinger. *The Charlotte Observer,* April 1, 1994.

About the Author

Clark Cox has been a reporter and editor on weekly and small daily newspapers for 40 years. He presently is a senior writer for The Pilot, a thrice-weekly paper in Southern Pines. Cox, a native of Jefferson, N.C., grew up in the North Carolina mountains and was a Morehead scholar at the University of North Carolina at Chapel Hill. He now lives in Rockingham, N.C., with his wife, Helen, and two children, Candice and Tom.

He has won numerous awards in newspaper work and local history. He has written or edited two books of local history, a book of family history, a published short story that has been adapted for televison, and two plays that were produced by local companies.

He is a Kentucky colonel and has been a deacon in his church. In his spare time, Cox enjoys reading, movies and watching baseball.

High Country Publishers, Ltd

invites you to our website to learn more about High Country Publishers and other High Country Publishers' books. Read exerpts and reviews from books by other authors. Learn what's new at High Country Publishers. Link to other authors' sites, preview upcoming titles, and find out how you can order books at a discount for your group or organization.

www.highcountrypublishers.com

High Country Publishers, Ltd

Boone, NC
2003